MW00439800

PRAISE FOR ELLEN POOLE AND *"NETWORK" IS NOT A VERB*

"Networks are essential for success and progress for all of us, individually and in all aspects of our life. *"Network" Is Not A Verb* helps all of us to grow up and realize that there is no one alone involved in any meaningful progress. Ellen Poole helps us all to find the trailhead on the map of moving forward with the network you need."

— *Dr. Michael M. Crow*
President, Arizona State University,
U.S. News & World Report's *"#1 most innovative school" six years in a row*

"While reading Ellen's book, I found myself having multiple 'ah ha' moments as I reflected on my own experiences in the corporate leadership world. I also laughed out loud at some of the real-life practical lessons that too often I learned the hard way! Her refreshing approach creates an easy roadmap no matter where you are along your career or personal path to developing and sustaining a business network that can also be a network of life-long friends!"

— *Starlette B. Johnson*
Former President & COO of Dave & Buster's, Inc.;
former Chief Strategic Officer, Brinker International;
current Board Member, Virginia Tech Foundation, Inc.

"This book is a must read for anyone seeking practical and effective methods for building and growing a rewarding and beneficial network. Ellen shares amazing real-world tips and genuine techniques for enhancing and enjoying productive, authentic relationships in your professional and personal life for the mutual success of all involved."

— *Donna Davis*
Former Regional Administrator, U.S. Small Business Administration;
small business owner

"NETWORK" IS NOT A VERB

ELLEN POOLE

"NETWORK" IS NOT A VERB

The Authentic Way to Build Meaningful
Professional Relationships for Lifetime Success

ELLEN POOLE

Foreword by Wayne Peacock – President & CEO, USAA

All rights reserved. No part of this book may be reproduced or transmitted in any form or by any means, electronic or mechanical, including photography, recording or in any information storage or retrieval system without written permission from the author and publisher. The scanning, uploading, or distribution of this book or parts thereof without permission is a theft of the owner's intellectual property.

If you purchase this book without a cover you should be aware that this book may have been stolen property and reported as "unsold and destroyed" to the publisher. In such case neither the author nor the publisher has received any payment for this "stripped book." This publication is designed to provide competent and reliable information regarding the subject matter covered. However, it is sold with the understanding that the author and publisher are not engaged in rendering legal, financial, or other professional advice. Laws and practices often vary from state to state and country to country and if legal or other expert assistance is required, the services of a professional should be sought. The author and publisher specifically disclaim any liability that is incurred from the contents of this book or its use or application.

Copyright © 2021 by Ellen Poole. All rights reserved. Except as permitted under the U.S. Copyright Act of 1976, no part of this publication may be reproduced, distributed, or transmitted in any form or by any means or stored in a database for retrieval.

Published by Brisance Books Group LLC.

The publisher is not responsible for websites or their content that are not owned by the publisher.

Brisance Books Group LLC
21001 N. Tatum Blvd.
Suite 1630
Phoenix, AZ 85050

Printed in the United States of America

First Edition: April 2021

Hardcover

ISBN: 978-1-944194-78-9

Jacket photo: Stewart Jones – Focus First Photography

Cover design: PCI Publishing Group

072021

"Try not to become a man of success,
but rather try to become a man of value."

— Albert Einstein

TABLE OF CONTENTS

FOREWORD

by Wayne Peacock, President & CEO, USAA

When my friend Ellen Poole approached me about writing the foreword for this book, I instantly agreed.

Many years ago, USAA committed to build a significant regional campus in Phoenix. Major projects like this are invariably complex, with a host of potential obstacles and a litany of required prerequisites and permissions. Hard work and helpful relationships are invaluable when it comes to navigating such complexities. And Ellen, who then was a USAA government-affairs executive, was a pro. Over the years, her confident competence and congenial advocacy had allowed her to assemble an unsurpassed network of public and private-sector professionals in Arizona. Those relationships and Ellen's diligence and talent made her indispensable to our success.

Like so many others who have worked or socialized with Ellen, I have never forgotten her capability, professionalism and warmth. It's been almost two decades since we brought the Phoenix campus to life and several years since Ellen left USAA to start her own consulting firm. Yet we are still connected by those bonds formed long ago.

Her book is honest with sensible messages that deserve to be heard and amplified. "I believe the world would function more smoothly and be a more delightful place," Ellen writes, "if everyone were to create and nurture *relationships*, instead of spending time 'networking.'" I couldn't agree more.

"Networking" – a term she disdains – too often treats relationships as transactional – mere tools to be exploited for personal gain. A cottage industry has sprung up of "expert consultants" who aim to convince us that our careers will crumble if we don't collect enough business cards – as though relationships were trophies and connections were only currency. That shallow, disingenuous pursuit is inauthentic at its core, Ellen argues. Building relationships must be more than a means to an end. Richer relationships, she teaches, will open doors not just to career advancement and business success, but to *life* success – to a fuller enjoyment of our entire human experience.

Ellen is well qualified to evangelize this better way. She has enjoyed a remarkably successful career as a lobbyist and influencer by forging authentic relationships. And over time, others who admired her success began to seek her out for advice. This book is full of her wisdom and sensibility: Find opportunities to show your value. Be genuinely interested in others (and be interesting yourself). Make yourself memorable by finding and reinforcing common ground with new acquaintances. And, at the foundation of the advice architecture, there is this: To be good at building a network, begin by being very good at your job – not just competent, but indispensable and eager to help and serve others.

Indeed, this service mindset is immensely powerful not just for individuals, but also for companies. At USAA, helping our members in the military community find financial security is our mission and the soul of our culture. We know what it means to serve. And the depth of our employees' empathy-driven member relationships led to USAA being labeled "The Most Beloved Financial Brand on Earth." Those genuine relationships are the reason why we consistently rank atop so many customer-experience ratings. They are the reason why we have earned a fierce loyalty unrivaled in the financial-services industry. And they are the reason why those we serve are more likely to recommend us to friends than almost any other American company in *any* industry.

If you aspire to have rich, reciprocal and loyal relationships, you will find practical advice in these pages to help you evolve. You will discover pointers for remembering defining details about new acquaintances, and ideas about how to follow up to reinforce your new connections. You will learn the difference between asking someone to coffee and asking them to lunch – and why the latter is a much bigger risk. And you will gain how-to advice on matters such as starting conversations with strangers, as well as how to bring a graceful end to a conversation that has run its course.

Reading *"Network" Is Not a Verb* is like meeting a new and long-sought mentor. Heed this book's guidance and master these skills and you just might find that others in your relationship circles will be seeking out *your* mentorship.

"NETWORK" IS NOT A VERB

It's who you know. Haven't you heard that a million times in your life? It starts early when a college classmate gets that great job and someone mutters that his uncle's golf buddy owns the company. Throughout your working life you hear it when someone else lands that promotion or gets hired for the position you thought was a sure thing for *you*. When a competitor makes the big sale, people nod knowingly and say, of course they got it—it's all about who you know.

If it's who you know, then it necessarily follows that you must get to know more people, right? In fact, the more people the better! This has become such a core belief in our culture that the word "network," originally only a noun, now functions as a verb. It has inspired a cottage industry of events and groups convened for the sole purpose of meeting other people so they can help you get ahead. Go-getters refer in conversation to their monthly "networking groups." Conferences that used to be considered opportunities to expand professional knowledge now are attended solely in order to "network," with educational sessions inconveniently interrupting the "networking" activities. Time between the sessions to use the restroom or check your messages has been relabeled on agendas as "networking breaks."

At the same time, advice from so-called "networking" experts has begun to permeate business media. People who devote time to "networking" are viewed by others as being more on the ball professionally and more likely to get ahead. Those who don't "network" feel uneasy that they are somehow falling behind by not devoting attention to this essential activity. And all these beliefs are reinforced every time anyone loses a promotion, a sale or a deal that went to someone else—they didn't know the right person, so they'd better start "networking."

The reality, however, is that "networking" at events and conferences never has been an effective way to build successful relationships with colleagues and friends. Think back on "networking" events you attended. Wasn't participation in these activities generally unsatisfying? You attended the gatherings, handed out your business cards and collected those of others, but did it ever really do any good? If you are an introvert, as I am, these activities even verged at times on painful—all that forced socializing with strangers.

I recently was going through a stack of business cards I'd collected over the past year at several conferences that I attended on behalf of a client. My purpose at the conferences wasn't to "network" but instead to educate people about my client's product through conversations at receptions and during breaks from educational sessions. Nevertheless, I accumulated a ton of business cards from the people I talked to, and that was the stack I was belatedly going through.

I threw away 80 percent of the cards I had collected because I couldn't remember the people who gave them to me. Even though at the time I had written something on each card about the person or the circumstance in which I met them, I still drew a blank on most of them. Others went in the trash when I realized that, even though I vaguely remembered the person, he or she would have to comb their memories with bloodhounds and a searchlight before recollecting *me*.

Had I gone to these conferences with the aim of "networking," they would have been a waste of time and money. The truth is that conventions, conferences, and typical "networking" events are not and never have been places to build lasting relationships. They might be great places for a serendipitous "sale," *if* you meet a person who at that particular moment in time is looking to acquire what you have to offer (yourself for a job? A contract with your company? A new office copier?), or vice versa. They also can provide opportunities to cement relationships you already have. But otherwise, once you go home it is rare to continue any kind of future connection with the majority of people you met. Six months later you, like me, are tossing a pile of business cards into the circular file.

The other problem with "networking" is that many people just don't enjoy it. They fear they are not good at it. They think they will have to be "fake" in order to succeed. Despite the plethora of books encouraging introverted people that they too can "network," it's a fact that being outgoing and extroverted is a major advantage in traditional "networking" scenarios. Many people dread what they see as the superficial chitchat that is the stuff of convention and "networking" event conversations.

Other people are willing but just can't fit it into their schedules. A proliferation of "networking" experts advise daily "networking" calls, or attendance at two weekly "networking" events, or an hour each day updating contacts, or heaven forbid, "curating" your own "networking" group. People tend to throw up their hands. Who has *time* to do all this? Who even wants to? Because of the core belief that "who you know" is critical to success, however, people persevere in these activities, uneasy at the thought of being left out and uncomfortable with abandoning the idea of "networking" altogether.

These kinds of experiences illustrate why "networking" is generally wasted effort. The activities are time consuming, potentially expensive, often unpleasant, and it is difficult to pin down any actual benefit. And yet somehow there are people who seem to naturally build great professional relationships and enjoy networks of contacts that benefit them in multiple ways. I refuse to "network," but I have built a web of relationships that has been critical to my life's success, both personally and professionally. I have made great friends, enjoyed incredible, one-of-a-kind experiences, and achieved a challenging and rewarding career.

It's only now, though, after more than thirty years of achievement in the workplace and having made my living for much of that time as a lobbyist for whom relationships are a necessity, that I can look back and see how my ability to organically build authentic work relationships aided me. For me these skills came instinctively from the beginning. I remember in one early worker-bee job in pre-computer days being tasked regularly with delivering documents to other company departments. Each of these errands, which should have taken only a few moments, would last fifteen minutes or longer as I would get into conversations with the documents' recipients, fascinated to learn about their careers and interests. One day the head of our department came into my little cubbyhole to tell me he'd heard I was friendly with the head of the PR division, whom I'd gotten to know as I made my rounds. Would I be willing to ask him to help our team with a difficult project? It turned out that I, the lowest person on the totem pole in our department, was the only person who knew the guy more than just to say hello to. I had begun building my network and didn't even know it.

In the years since then, my ability to build a strong network has brought me professional success and personal rewards. I haven't applied for a job in more than twenty-five years—every professional opportunity that has come my way has been the result of people in my network reaching out to *me*. I have had enriching personal experiences as well. I have been hosted for lunch at the White House, cheered Olympic figure skating from the second row of the arena, petted a rhinoceros at the Honolulu Zoo, and witnessed a rocket launch up close because of the wonderful opportunities shared with me by friends in my network.

When I was working as an executive in government relations at a large corporation, a company colleague who led a customer service team called one day and asked if I'd give an update at their next regular team meeting about the state legislature's activities. "Ok," I replied dubiously, "but it's gonna last about five minutes—there's nothing happening this time of year." "Well then talk about 'networking,'" she suggested. She continued by saying that she was frustrated with her people's inability to get to know anyone beyond the cubicle next to theirs. I agreed to do so, and the night before the meeting I sat down to try to organize speaking points on something that was an instinctive part of my life and to which I had never before given much thought.

I spoke to her team, and they told other colleagues how much they had enjoyed my presentation. Soon I was being asked to speak to larger and larger groups at my company. As those people mentioned my remarks to friends outside of work, I began to get requests from other organizations. The principles I spoke about seemed so basic to me, yet were eagerly received by my audiences. As I spoke to more and more groups, I worked to polish my presentations and really crystalize my thoughts about how my approach to building relationships had been integral to my achievements. And when I reflected on my own experiences, I had to admit one thing: I hated "networking."

As someone others considered a star "networker," this was a revelation. The title of my speech was "networking," but the relationship-building advice I offered had nothing to do with shaking hands or conversation over a stuffed mushroom. Traditional "networking" was something I disliked, felt disdain for, and avoided where at all possible. Even to this day, at the end of a typical convention dinner and keynote speaker, no one leaps to their feet to exit the room more quickly than I do. In fact, I am back in my hotel room in my pajamas with my novel before the rest of the crowd has ordered its first round of after-dinner drinks in the bar. On the rare occasion I force myself to attend a "networking" event, I spend inordinate amounts of time in the restroom and leave as soon as it won't appear rude. Despite these aversions, however, I have been nurtured and supported by a wonderful web of professional colleagues throughout my life. How had I created this network of valuable and meaningful connections?

That is why I wrote this book. I want others to enjoy the same support and beneficial relationships as I have. I believe the world would function more smoothly and be a more delightful place if everyone were to create and nurture relationships, instead of spending time "networking." It is rewarding and uplifting to engage with someone who adopts this approach to life and to relating and communicating with other people. Furthermore, you do not have to be outgoing, possessed of a sparkling personality, or be willing to devote tens or hundreds of hours a year to artificial "networking" events. I believe that anyone can do it.

THE CORE PRINCIPLE

If "networking" is not the answer, what is? How do you organically create worthwhile connections with friends and colleagues for lifelong mutual support? There is one Core Principle that must guide your approach to your professional relationships. **To successfully build your own meaningful network you must *be* someone whom others wish to have in THEIR networks.** In other words, you must offer value to other people so that they want to add you to their own circle of contacts.

This simple but timeless principle has always been the essential means by which to build relationships and develop your network. Effective implementation is just as possible today as it has been in the last twenty or even fifty years. You don't have to attend time-consuming, expensive or stressful "networking" events. You don't have to be extroverted, insincere, or anyone other than yourself.

By following my ten Tactical Tips, you can build your network by adopting the Core Principle and forging value-based relationships as you go about your own "best life." And I'm going to show you how to do it.

THE PERFORMANCE FACTOR

TIP #1:

BE GOOD AT YOUR JOB

There. I've said it. You don't even need the rest of this book; close it, take it back to the bookstore, and maybe they will give you a refund. Just by being good at your job you can go forth and build all the relationships you will ever need. This is the single most important step to creating a rewarding network of supportive relationships.

In all the speeches I've given on relationship building, I often look out at the audience before I begin and see them waiting to take notes. There is always a look of surprise, even shock, on faces when I start with this tip as the primary basis for creating your professional network. Some people even put down their pens or sit back from their keyboards, puzzled.

But think about it for a moment. Who are the people you gravitate to at work? The ones who help you get things done. Who is the plumber you recommend? The one who came to your house right away and quickly stopped your water heater leak. In any circumstance, don't you love the person who handles something the first time so that you don't have to call them back several days later?

Those people are building their own networks every day just by being great at their jobs. And if you want to build a fantastic network, the first thing you need to do is ask yourself if you are doing your job as well as you could be. Interestingly, for most people, what holds them back here is not an absence of genius. Now, I'm not knocking genius. Everyone wants to know and be known by the people who are absolutely the best in their fields. And oftentimes those people can get away with mediocre professional behavior that would sink the rest of us. You need to do the best work you can, no question, and if you can get to the top of your profession, you will have a fantastic network the rest of your days. But what about the rest of us average folk? There are two critical things we can do in our jobs that will demonstrate our value and cause others to automatically add us to *their* networks.

First, most people think about being good at their jobs from their employer's perspective. Does the boss think they are doing quality work? Are they checking the boxes in their job description? Was the last performance evaluation a complimentary one? It's definitely a good thing if the answer to these questions is yes. But that's not the kind of "good at your job" I'm talking about. I'm telling you to be good at your job *from the perspective of the people with whom you come into contact every day as you go about your ordinary work.* You need to be good at your job in a way that **solves their problems**. Everyone wants to have relationships with the people who can do that for them! So often, however, we are caught up in our own little worlds, focused on doing our "job duties." We rarely take a moment to look at our work from the other person's viewpoint and truly understand what that person is looking for from us. What problem are they wanting us to solve?

I once admired a model sailboat in a hotel gift shop while on a vacation in San Diego, but it was large and I would have had difficulty getting it home to Arizona, so I decided not to buy it. As soon as I got home from the trip, of course, I kicked myself for not purchasing it. I called the hotel and asked to be transferred to the gift shop. The salesperson who answered the phone was very pleasant. She was so sorry, but the shop's policy was not to ship items. Could she at least tell me where they had gotten the item, I asked. "Hmmm, no... ," she couldn't. She apologized again, and ended the call.

Undeterred, I called the hotel again and asked for the hotel concierge (I can be persistent). I told her about the conversation with the gift shop clerk and my regret at not buying the model during my stay. She told me she would look into it and call me back. Ten minutes later my phone rang. The concierge had gone into the store and set the item aside so it would not be bought by someone else before she could talk to the shop manager. Meanwhile, the concierge had examined the item closely, found the name of the manufacturer, and done an online search to see if the item was available anywhere else. She had located one in a store near my home. "Might that be a better alternative and less costly than shipping from out of state?" she asked. Thrilled, I thanked her and told her it was. I headed to the local store the following day. When I walked in and told the store clerk what I was looking for, she already knew. The concierge had called her and asked that the item be set aside for me.

I sent the concierge a thank you note and a gift card and told her if she ever needed a job reference to call me. I tracked down the names of her manager and the hotel manager and wrote both of them emails about how terrific she had been. For the next *year* I told everyone I knew who went to San Diego that they should stay in that hotel—because of the concierge.

By virtue of her job performance she had added me to her network. Was what she had done difficult? Not really, but unlike the gift shop clerk, she had focused on what I really wanted: to obtain the sailboat. Instead of getting all bound up in the gift shop's rules, or passing the buck to the manager, she figured out how to help me by finding the sailboat for me in my home town. The gift shop clerk was too focused on "doing her job" (pleasantly answering questions on the phone) to really see my problem and ask herself what she could do to help solve it. The concierge, on the other hand, saw my problem and fixed it, and by doing so she identified herself to me as a valuable person to know. She therefore added me to her own network of people she could call on for help.

Listen, there is no question that you absolutely must be competent at the substance of your work in order to succeed. I don't care what you do for a living: If you are a bad lawyer, bad manager, bad hair stylist—whatever— the broadest network in the world won't help you. I am reminded of someone I knew many years ago. At the time, she had a high-powered job that put us into the same professional circles, and we became friendly. She was outgoing and pleasant, a dedicated "networker," and seemed to be liked by everyone. When she lost that job because of what appeared to be internal politics, she turned to her extensive network of contacts to help her find new employment. Although many of us tried to help, a string of jobs followed from which she was successively fired. Despite her personal charm, it turned out that she simply was not very competent. She had obtained the first job through a connection, but performed poorly. As she was quickly let go from each of the jobs her network helped her find (complaining each time about the bad boss, unpleasant responsibilities, or demeaning duties), her friends—myself included—began to conclude that recommending her would not reflect well on *us*. Last I heard she was unemployed yet again.

If you are competent at your work, however, your standout ability to solve problems on the job is the number one reason people will want to know you and include you in their networks. This in turn will mean that they are in yours. The hotel concierge would have been one hundred percent correct, for example, had she told friends that she could get job search assistance from a lawyer in Arizona.

Practice looking at the requests and assignments that come your way through the eyes of the person who gave them to you. What do they really need or want to happen, even if they didn't express it that way? If you were trying to do *their* job, what would you want from you? How can you do your work to make their lives easier?

I once was lobbying against a difficult piece of legislation that, although well-intentioned, would have added numerous steps to my company's process for handling insurance claims. Brainstorming for ways to show lawmakers why this was a bad proposal, I came up with a clever idea. I asked one of my company's data analysts for a chart showing how much increased time it would take for our customers to receive their claims payments if this legislation were to pass. In response, the analyst sent me two documents—the chart I asked for *and* a chart showing the added financial cost to the customer for each extra day he had to wait for payment. This problem-solver really listened and heard what I *needed*— information that would show why the legislation would harm our company's customers—instead of only what I asked for. He then used his expertise to provide me with the best information that would help me do *my* job. Conclusion? The legislation was defeated and this rock star analyst and I added each other to our networks of valuable contacts.

Examples abound. Just recently I submitted to a client a complicated invoice that got stuck somewhere in the bill-paying process. When a few months went by and a check still had not appeared, my client was mortified. He called his company's Accounts Payable department several times, but nothing happened. Each successive week we both became more frustrated with my empty mailbox. Finally one day he called me and announced, "I found The Person." "Who?" I asked. "The Person," he said, "Who Gets Things Done in Accounting." He had connected with a woman in the department who heard the problem, quickly figured out the system glitch that was preventing the check from being issued, processed the payment, then actually printed the check, put it in the envelope herself, and walked it to the mailbox. Problem solved. My client now goes straight to her any time he needs anything from Accounts Payable, and he raves about her to anyone who will listen. If she applies for a promotion, will he recommend her? You bet. Can you be "The Person" in your world? It doesn't take genius, it takes effort.

The second way to be good at your job to enhance the likelihood that others will see your value and want to add you to their networks is to *not* do something. That is, do *not* do the little things that irritate and frustrate people so that they think of you as less capable than you are. The reality is that we all constantly subconsciously evaluate the professional quality of the people around us. There are many people we may like personally but who have shortcomings in the workplace. How often have you said something like, "He's really nice, but he's always late," or, "She's very smart, but she is really bad about getting back to people"? How about

"He's so funny, but he's always horribly unprepared in meetings"? Do not give people a reason to say "but..." about you!

I once worked with a colleague who was smart and had really instinctive insight into politics. But, she never got back to *anyone*. Others at our company, knowing we were in the same department, would complain regularly about her to me; one co-worker memorably said that sending her an email was like dropping a rock into a thousand-foot well—you had no idea when or if it hit bottom. Ouch. Despite this colleague's superior abilities she was not well thought of, because she frustrated people who needed something from her to do their jobs. Interestingly, when she finally left the company, she seemed to struggle in finding a new position. Meanwhile her replacement, who actually was less qualified than she, was responsive and had a helpful attitude, and his co-workers loved him.

Could you be better at getting back to people quickly so they don't have to bug you on Friday about something you said you'd do by Tuesday? Could you show up to meetings and appointments on time, instead of always rushing in five or ten minutes late? Could you even come in to work five minutes early, or stay at work until ten after? Even if you looked in the mirror this morning and ruefully acknowledged to yourself that you are just average, these are easy things you can do to create an overall impression of competence. More importantly, they will help you avoid negative judgments from those who might otherwise see your special value as a problem solver.

You may be saying to yourself, "This is great advice for when I finally get a job in my ideal field. But right now, I'm just waiting tables to make ends meet." Au contraire—**there is no better time to begin following Tip #1 and putting the advice in this chapter to work.** First, many of your restaurant co-workers may be thinking the same thing, which means that it will be easier for you to stand out from the crowd than it will be later when you join other go-getters scrabbling for success in your dream career. Second, as we will further explore later on, you never know who will be important in your life. The grateful restaurant manager whose stress you relieved when you stayed for a second, unscheduled shift on a busy night will remain in your network for many years to come.

Stop looking at your job performance as relevant only to your boss' view of you. The reality is that everyone at work is watching you, and they are judging and evaluating you based on their experience with you. If you solve their problems they will rave about you and want to have a relationship with you. And unconsciously they are including you in their networks... or not.

PUTTING IT INTO PRACTICE

Having concrete examples from our past experiences often helps solidify ideas about how we can apply a principle in the future. At the end of each chapter, I'll ask you to come up with your own examples and note your thoughts about how you can put what you learn in this book into practice now and in the future.

Part of doing something new is being **reminded** *to do it—it's easy to forget to do something a new way when we are used to doing it the old way. Some of the practice ideas will suggest creating a checklist or putting time on your calendar specifically for this purpose. If you have other techniques that help you to remember to do something or create and anchor new habits, I encourage you to use those as well.*

PUTTING IT INTO PRACTICE
TIP #1 – Be Good at Your Job

Past: *Identify an example of Tip #1 in action from your life. Maybe someone was extravagantly appreciative of something you did at work that really helped them. Perhaps you've observed someone else following Tip #1: One of your colleagues is everyone's go-to person, or you were the lucky individual whose problem was solved by someone you've worked with.*

Present: *What are you working on **right now** in your job or business where you could step up your game and "go the extra mile" on a project or a request?*

Future: *Set 15 minutes in your calendar every Monday morning to review everything you are working on and identify what the other people **really** need from you — not just what they said they needed — and how you can problem-solve for them. Make a list where you check off daily the "easy" things we talked about in Chapter One, if those are areas where you could use improvement. Some ideas for your checklist include: a) arrive for meetings five minutes before they start; b) answer all your email requests within 48 hours with either a substantive reply or a note letting the sender know you got it and you'll be working on it; c) block time in your calendar, even just 15 minutes, to prepare in advance for meetings.*

MAKING AN IMPRESSION

TIP #2:

BE INTERESTING

I know, you just rechecked the cover of this book to make sure that you didn't accidentally buy a book about dating. But the reality is, people in your professional network will relish knowing you more if you are interesting. Your own life feels enriched when you know people who do unusual or interesting things, does it not? Also, interesting people are easier to remember after you meet them. If you are trying to get to know someone, it is a major stumbling block if they can't remember you once the conversation is over.

So here's your Tip: Develop your hobbies and interests. This benefits you in three ways. First, if you do interesting things, you have something interesting to talk about, and people will remember you the next time they encounter you and will enjoy talking with you. Second, when you encounter another enthusiast of your particular hobby, you will bond with that person and accelerate the development of that relationship. Third, isn't life about more than your job and your obligations? You'll be a happier person if you spend time on the things you enjoy. Not everything is about work, people!

I love figure skating and skated recreationally for many years before a bad knee sidelined me. I dabbled in ice dance (at a low skill level—trust me, I did not forego an Olympic career for law school), and enthusiastically participated on the administrative side of things, helping to put on local competitions and fundraisers and eventually becoming president of my local skating club.

People in my work world who learned about this hobby found it very interesting and often wanted to talk with me about skating. When I worked as a peon on state legislative staff, one February the big-deal President of the Senate called me and asked me to come to his office immediately. I quickly raced from my basement office to the second floor for what I thought was an urgent policy meeting. The actual subject? He and his wife were avidly watching the Olympic skating competition every evening and he wondered who I thought would take the Ladies' Figure Skating gold medal.

During that same time, another lawmaker who knew of my love for skating retired from the legislature. Seventeen years went by, and then she was reelected and returned to public office. By then I was a lobbyist, and I took part in a large meeting with her in a crowded conference room. As we went around the room introducing ourselves she nodded politely as each person spoke, but when it came my turn she said, "Oh yes, you're the skater."

Your hobbies don't have to be glamorous or high-powered. I have met and enjoyed talking with people whose interests included canning fruit preserves, visiting major league ballparks, collecting rare books, working as a volunteer EMT, training dogs, French cooking, and riding roller coasters. In fact, depending on the situation, a high-powered hobby can work against you. I remember once talking to a bank president who told me that he and his family enjoyed heli-skiing. My unsophisticated self had to ask what it was. For those of you not in the know, it's where a helicopter—in his case the family helicopter—takes you to the top of an otherwise-inaccessible mountain so that you can ski down. While certainly memorable, it made my own interests seem a little pedestrian. He and I clearly weren't going to bond over heli-skiing. Naturally, I wanted him to be part of *my* network, but he wasn't going to connect with me based on shared interests, although I could at least listen enthusiastically. Luckily I was following Tip #1 and being good at my job—which worked, by the way.

Even a simple food preference can help you connect with someone with whom you have little else in common. I don't care for other desserts, but love ice cream and will eat it any chance I get. Over ice cream, I developed a friendship with a reserved, state legislator from rural Colorado who ultimately became the President of the Colorado State Senate. While sitting in my assigned seat next to this quiet man at a chamber of commerce luncheon, ice cream was unexpectedly served for dessert (a rarity, since typically desserts at big luncheons tend to be those that don't melt while waiting to be served). I noticed that he wasn't touching his and asked him if I could have it. That led to a discussion of ice cream in general, and a promise on my part to treat him to an ice cream cone the next time I was in town. Seven years and dozens of ice cream cones later, we are unlikely but fast friends: The quiet, conservative rural grandfather from Colorado and the talkative lawyer lobbyist from Arizona.

If you are quiet by nature, having an interesting story or hobby helps you stand out in a group. I served on a trade association board with a number of people who were loud and talkative; we had all become friends after being on this board together for several years. One year a new, shy young lady joined our board. We were all friendly and pleasant toward her, but she was quiet and did not stand out in this ebullient crowd.

A few months later we had our annual board of directors retreat, and the executive director began with an ice breaker in which we went around the room and told the group something unusual or memorable about ourselves. People told different stories, some more (or less) interesting than others. When it was this woman's turn, she told us that on a high school trip to France she and a couple of classmates had physically tackled and detained an international terrorist who happened to be fleeing an attempted attack just as she and her friends were walking by. Our jaws dropped. For the rest of the retreat, this quiet person did not have to initiate a single conversation; every chance we got we gathered around to hear more details of this amazing story. From that day on, she was no longer the shy one; she was the terrorist capturer, and utterly memorable.

Being interesting is not enough to offset a failure to show value, or worse, professional incompetence. Never forget that all roads lead back to Tip #1 – be good at your job. But being interesting is a value-add. It makes people want to know you more, and it makes people enjoy talking with you as they get to know you. Remember my story about my early days delivering documents around the building? I myself was pretty boring back then, but I loved hearing about why my recipients were interesting, and that is why they liked talking with me. I remember to this day that the public relations director was restoring a cherry-red, classic Corvette, and I would ask for an update on it whenever I stopped by with a sheaf of papers.

Look, most of us love to talk about our hobbies and interests to others who are good listeners. In those conversations we tend to sparkle. We don't struggle to find words or fill awkward pauses. If you can be that person, and let someone else be that person in conversation with you, you will naturally enhance your relationship.

One closing caveat regarding this Tip. Your children's activities do not make *you* interesting. By all means, if you are so inclined, share your joy in your children with your friends and colleagues, but do not use your kids' hobbies and interests as a way to be memorable or bond with new acquaintances. There are several reasons this is a bad idea. First, most children's activities are not unique. Soccer games, internships, high school plays—no matter how wonderful your child is at these pursuits, they are typical of many childhoods. Second, even if you are talking to someone whose child participates in the same activity as yours does, there is a subtle distinction in the nature of the relationship that is formed. To one another you are primarily a *parent*, not an individual with your own professional identity. While this may help you put together a carpool, it generally will not advance your career or create professional opportunities for you. Finally, even if your child's activities are so outstanding as to be fascinating, like those of the child of a woman I met recently—her daughter graduated high school, within a week was cast in a major motion picture, and is now a famous movie actor—the person listening is mentally comparing your offspring to his or her little Susie and is worried that Susie is coming up short. This can actually create a barrier between you and the other person. You also risk coming off as smug and a braggart. Best not to go there.

PUTTING IT INTO PRACTICE
TIP #2 – Be Interesting

Past: *Think of someone you've known who had a hobby that made you find that person more interesting or enjoyable to talk to. If you have ever had a hobby or passion that you engaged in outside of work, recall occasions when other people asked about it, or times you mentioned it and co-workers were interested.*

Present: *What hobby or interest are you enjoying **right now** that you could talk about in casual conversation or when people ask you about yourself?*

Future: *Identify a hobby that's always intrigued you that you've never had time to pursue. Check out the Internet for classes, clubs, or meet-up groups in your area. Maybe you have a friend who wants to join you in exploring this new activity. Or, instead of a hobby, maybe there's a subject you've always wanted to learn about. Take a class, watch a movie, or buy a book and start reading.*

BROADENING YOUR REACH

TIP #3:

FIND NEW PLACES TO SHOW VALUE

Tip #1 (Be good at your job) and Tip #2 (Be interesting) are about how to conduct yourself to be a valuable member of someone else's network. But now let's talk about how to meet people outside of work with whom you can build relationships. This is what people normally think of and do when they decide to invest time in "networking," right? You may be thinking, "Enough of being interesting and working hard; I want to go to receptions and hand out business cards!"

Remember my point at the beginning of this book, though: "Networking" events, those ubiquitous social functions that permeate the business world, are not the way to build a network of meaningful relationships. If such a network is your goal, receptions or lunches where you mingle with other people who are looking to "network" are a waste of time. If you paid to get in, they are also a waste of money. At those events, everyone mills around hoping to meet someone who will benefit *them*. Attendees dutifully follow the advice of "networking" experts, such as "identify important targets to talk to," "hand out at least three business cards" and "use the person's name in the conversation as you are speaking."

The whole goal is to somehow entice the people you are meeting into wanting to do business with you, or help you get a job, or provide one of any other benefits they can give *you*. **But this is going about it backward.** No one—including you—goes to these occasions thinking about meeting people in terms of what value the *other* person is looking for.

It is unlikely that most of us in a brief conversation can show someone else the kind of value that makes them want to build a relationship with us. You're the CEO of Google? Then everyone who meets you wants you in their network. The rest of us, however, must find opportunities to demonstrate our value, so that others seek us out. You do this not through "networking" events, but by joining organizations and participating in their activities.

A few thoughts before you join. Here is the paradox: Any organization can be a good forum to build your network, but you must choose carefully the organizations in which you plan to participate. Wait a minute, you ask... if any organization works, then why do I have to choose carefully? **Because you are going to be working hard once you get there, and it should be worth your time, energy, and resources.**

Choose an organization or two that have purposes you think will be good for you professionally or personally regardless of the number of "contacts" you make. Do some research in advance. If you know someone who is a member, talk to him about it and find out what it's really like. See if the group is mentioned online or has a website. If possible, attend a meeting or activity. Remember: You are attending this event *not* to "network" but to learn more about the group and determine whether it is for you. Are the attendees the types of people with whom you would like to build long-term relationships? Will you learn something by participating?

Will it be fun or at least engaging enough so that you will gladly put in effort over a long period of time once the newness fades?

Once you have chosen your target groups, you must approach the club, association, etc. with a different mindset from the "networking" one you may have had in the past. This is critical: Instead of joining to see who you can meet there that will be beneficial to *you*, you now will be joining to show how you can benefit *them*. Basically, you are finding new people to whom to demonstrate your mastery of Tips #1 and #2 – you are good at what you do and you are interesting.

In order to do this, you *must* be a terrific member of any group you join. You must treat it seriously; a casual attitude about membership will result in failure. Apply the principles we've discussed regarding your paying job. Show up to all meetings and events. Come early and stay late. Prepare by reviewing relevant materials before attending; follow through on action items you offer to undertake, even just simple ones like looking for a cooler in your garage to bring to the annual 5K charity event. Volunteer to help with *everything*. Your goal is to work your way into a leadership role (board member or officer, annual fundraiser leader, Fourth of July picnic organizer, committee chair, etc.). Some organizations are thrilled to have any new member take a top role immediately; in other places these positions are coveted and you will need to show over time that you are committed to the organization before you can get onto a leadership track.

You are doing all of this for two reasons. First, by working hard and demonstrating responsibility, you will be held in high esteem by your fellow members. Recall any club or association you've joined before—you always knew who the "doers" were, right? If you play a leadership role, this benefit is magnified: Even more people within the organization can see firsthand that you are an asset to the group. You will be viewed positively by members whom you may not have gotten to know yet. This makes those people want to know *you*. They will begin to participate with the goal of getting to know *you* and adding you to their networks.

Second, when you work on an organization project, you build relationships with your fellow collaborators more effectively than if you just show up at the club's monthly meeting or, heaven forbid, "networking reception." Working on a project with a team brings people together. It creates opportunities for shared laughter and shared frustration. There may be final celebration of a job well done. All of this allows you to show people up close that you are reliable and capable. As anyone who has ever been an officer in a club knows, problems *will* arise, and this is your chance to solve them, thereby demonstrating your value to all of the other association members. By doing great work inside these organizations, people beyond those you meet at your job will learn that you would be a valuable member of their own networks. This way *you* are building relationships, but you are not "networking" at all. You are simply being fantastic at what you do for the organization.

You can do yourself irreparable harm, however, if you join an association, commit to participation, and then *don't* follow through. I once was embarrassed to receive a phone call from a government official asking for help with the following situation. A colleague at my company had received the honor of being appointed to a government agency advisory board, but in over a year had attended only one of the bimonthly meetings. The official apologized for bothering me, but asked if I could do anything to motivate the person into showing up. When I talked to my colleague, she explained that she had been on a business trip at the time of every meeting she had missed. To her that was a justifiable explanation for her absence. To the other members of the board, though, the conclusion was the same regardless of the reason: She appeared to be an unreliable person who didn't follow through on commitments. The irony was that she had accepted the appointment because she thought it would be good for her professionally. In reality, it harmed her reputation among the other industry colleagues on the board.

If you do not have the time to be a regular or active club or association member, **do not join**. This is why I recommend joining only one or two organizations—most people don't have the bandwidth to be rock stars at more than that. And do not think you will benefit if you join with the intention of participating only at the minimum level. Yes, you will avoid the worst sin of making commitments and then failing to follow through, but you will do nothing to build relationships. In the course of participating in a society or group, we all have been, at one point or another, in a conversation where a member's name comes up and the comment is made, "Oh, they never come." You do not want that said about you. If you can only rarely participate, why are you spending your resources?

I realize this does not apply to the many organizations we join for a specific reason. I am a member of the state bar, my homeowner's association, the United States Figure Skating Association, and my church. I've joined these for an acceptably limited purpose only—remaining licensed as a lawyer, mandatory membership by virtue of my home's location, receipt of the monthly skating magazine, and attendance at Sunday worship. These places do afford opportunity to build your network through active participation, and I would encourage you to evaluate your options there. You are already a member, so why not? But, they are the types of organizations that many people join for a limited benefit and therefore no negative light is cast upon the non-doers.

Another type of organization to consider is government boards and commissions. Your state, city or county probably has open seats on everything from the library commission to the parks board to the board of transportation. Many government boards are not comprised solely of experts on their subjects of oversight but include one or two members of the general public as well. Furthermore, these positions frequently are appointed from a slate of applicants who simply filled out an online form. Building relationships through these boards can be more of a long game, as their activities are likely to be very structured and subject to strict requirements, and your opportunities to shine will reveal themselves only over time. But if you have an interest in public policy or in building a network of people in the particular field, consider applying for a board or commission role. A caution here: My earlier recommendation to research the organization applies. Attend a meeting—many commission meetings are available for online viewing if you are uncomfortable going in person. Research the board on the internet, read minutes of past meetings and scan the bios of other members. Once again you are asking yourself: Is this an organization to which I want to dedicate time and resources?

Clubs or societies for members of your profession are often great places to become part of other people's networks if advancement within your own industry is uppermost in your mind. Demonstrating your abilities to competitors will expand your reputation in your industry far beyond your own employer. While those people won't know how good you are at your "day job," they are likely to enthusiastically recommend and embrace you as a future colleague at their own companies if they have seen firsthand your outstanding ability to get things done in a different context.

Don't ignore opportunities to join groups within your own company. If you work for a large employer, there are probably all kinds of extracurricular activities to join where you can deliver value to a cross-section of the company beyond your immediate team or department. Employee political action committee board? Mentoring team? Toastmasters? Corporate charitable activities? Look for opportunities to work on projects across multiple departments, or on which people from all over the company may volunteer.

As I write this book we are experiencing a trend toward virtual meetings and conference calls in lieu of in-person meetings. Never fear—these can provide opportunities to demonstrate your value to the group, so that people want to get to know you better in person. Nothing takes the place of face-to-face interaction to build a relationship, but at virtual meetings you can showcase your value to participants with whom you are not well-acquainted. A warning, however: Virtual meetings also can provide a venue to demonstrate negative qualities. While work-from-home circumstances can provide comical challenges for everyone, make a serious effort to minimize the barking dog or piles of dirty laundry in the background. Read and follow the advice of articles about creating a professional look and feel for these meetings with flattering lighting, attractive backgrounds and a quiet setting. Why take a chance that other participants have had a bad week and your wailing two-year-old is the last straw?

Try to show value in virtual meetings the same way you would in an in-person meeting. One benefit of online meetings is that the number of participants may be greater than is usual at your in-person gatherings, so there are more people to see you shine. Over the years my job has required conference calls with professionals in my industry from other states; upon subsequent face-to-face encounters, our relationships have been jumpstarted because I made a favorable impression beforehand.

A few tips on how to be viewed positively in a virtual meeting (as well as in an in-person meeting):

1. *Don't* be the person who never says anything. People can't tell whether you are even paying attention and they certainly won't remember you. Introverts, I know you'd prefer to not talk at all, but consider the stretch goal of trying to add one thought or comment every other meeting.

2. On the opposite end of the spectrum, unless it is required or you are asked, don't be the person who has to add his or her two cents to every single topic. I promise you that no matter how brilliant your contributions, people eventually will be rolling their eyes. Extroverts, this means you. If a talker like me can suppress this tendency, so can you.

3. *Try* not to say stupid things, although this one is hard to comply with 100 percent of the time. Just this week on a call I babbled on about a potential problem that I felt sure I was the only visionary who foresaw, only to be gently corrected by another caller that it had been solved before the call. Sigh. As I said, try.

4. If you do have to correct someone else, do it gently and kindly, so that the other person isn't embarrassed and it's not awkward for others in the meeting.

5. Don't argue with someone else on the call. A one-to-one disagreement is guaranteed to make everyone else uncomfortable. If your point is not getting across, just drop it politely and continue the discussion offline if you need to.

6. If you receive or volunteer for an assignment during the meeting, complete it quickly afterward and send an email to let the entire group know that it's done. This lets them witness your efficient follow-up skills. When you finally meet your online connections in person, they will be anxious to add you to their networks as a valuable colleague to have.

Back to organizations. What happens if you choose a group or two, begin to participate, and then realize that it's a bad fit? You don't like the people, or the activities are not what you hoped they would be. There is no shame in shifting gears or rethinking your decision. Organizations that look good from the outside may not turn out to be what you expected.

Many years ago I was lucky enough (I thought) to join a highly selective group of professionals that handled all the support activities for a college football bowl game. It was prestigious to be invited, and it sounded fun and worthwhile at the same time. Volunteers worked on the logistical aspects of putting on the game, which entailed a significant time commitment and therefore offered great opportunity to get to know and show value to fellow members.

Unfortunately, the membership back in those days seemed to consist primarily of good ol' boys who did not warmly welcome female newcomers. Despite not being socially inclusive toward me, though, they felt no restraint about approaching me for their own business benefit. For two-plus years I was the subject of relentless sales pitches by the many members who wanted business from my large corporate employer. I followed my own relationship-building precepts by faithfully attending meetings and volunteering, even co-chairing a major committee one year, but I finally called it quits. Conscious of my reputation to the end, I departed not by simply disappearing from the group but with a letter to the membership director. I thanked her for the wonderful opportunity but told her that other time commitments no longer allowed my participation.

A graceful departure is key. If you do join an organization that is a poor fit, or belong to one that no longer meets your needs or holds your interest, don't just allow your engagement to slowly peter out. Your reputation will take a hit if it is said about you, "He used to be on the board, but now he never does anything." All that work you did to build your network, negated! Instead, leave a lasting positive impression and maintain the relationships that you built there. Exit with a sincere letter to your colleagues thanking them but letting them know that you will no longer be a member. Much better if people comment about your departure, "It was a real blow to lose her."

Another point on joining organizations. This is so obvious it hardly bears mentioning, but you *must* be likeable and easy to get along with. You do not have to be the life of the party or even outgoing, but strive to be pleasant and friendly. Do not dig your heels in on decisions ("The T-shirts for this year's tennis tournament have to be green!") or get into arguments with fellow members about club matters. Don't be the person whose work is appreciated but whom everyone makes an excuse to avoid.

I recently was invited to join the prestigious board of an organization to which I had aspired for years. At my first meeting, I was shocked to see the board chair and several other members speak disparagingly to a fellow board member. Now that I've endured several meetings, however, I have observed that this board member is obsessed with a single issue that seems to be the only reason he is there. He brings up this issue whenever possible and then spends several minutes complaining about it. Despite efforts by the board to resolve his concern, he is never happy and tries to readdress the topic at every meeting. I now completely understand my fellow members' animosity toward this man. While I have made an effort to remain courteous toward this person, I have to admit my sympathies lie with my rude colleagues. Don't be this man.

A final point: As tempting as it may be, especially for those of you who are shy, do not become part of an internal clique, always sitting with or hanging out with the same three people. It may be a shortcut to feeling as though you belong, but you can easily alienate others who feel left out (remember junior high?). The reality is, that awkward newcomer feeling is experienced by everyone. To this day, even after all these years as a dedicated relationship builder, the first few meetings with a new group still trigger butterflies in my stomach. I have learned, though, that if I tough it out through the first two or three events, that feeling will disappear and I will begin to enjoy the group. People generally are friendly to newcomers. After all, most groups are always looking for help—new members, participants, or volunteers—and are glad to have you there. Even if they're not wildly welcoming, after two or three meetings you are a familiar face and people will treat you as though you belong there.

For your first few activities, choose brief ones. That way you know in advance that any discomfort will be of limited duration and you won't talk yourself out of going. I actually remind myself out loud before I head out the door that I'm likely to feel uneasy but that it's only an hour and soon I will be glad I joined.

Don't make the mistake I once made of undertaking an eight-hour hike as my first activity with a new hiking club. As nice as the people were, everyone there had been hiking together for many years and over the very looong day they naturally gravitated to conversations with other members with whom they had shared previous outdoor adventures. By the end of the day I was totally exhausted from trying to fit in. It would have been smarter of me to have joined a few hour-long hikes for my first forays into the group and built up to participating in larger doses.

The good news about any group is that eventually people who are newer than you will start coming, and *you* will get to be the old-timer who shows them the ropes. When that day comes, make sure you are nice and welcoming to the new people. Your kindness combined with your outstanding work will make them doubly anxious to add you to their networks right away.

Just remember: If you are someone who is uncomfortable in new groups, know that almost everyone else there felt that way when they started. That feeling will go away. Hang in there on this one, the payoffs are worth it.

PUTTING IT INTO PRACTICE
TIP #3 – Find New Places to Show Value

Past: *Think of any organizations or groups you've been part of in your life and recall the people there who impressed you. What did they do that made them stand out? While you are thinking this over and reflecting on positive examples, I suspect that names will also come to mind of people who let others down, or just never showed up.*

Present: *Are you a member of an organization, club, or extracurricular work team **right now**? If so, think of a way that you can volunteer for a leadership role of some kind. If you are already in a leadership role there, is there something extra you can do to go "above and beyond" in your current role and serve the other members?*

Future: *Make a list of organizations or work teams you've heard of that you would be interested in learning more about. Then, for the next few weeks, choose one each week to get more information on. If you know people who are involved, ask them about it. Research the groups on the Internet. If you don't know of any organizations that spark your interest, do a little research or ask around to find groups that are involved in activities that appeal to you. Once you've compiled a list of organizations that are potential targets, choose one to actually try out. Find out if you can go to a meeting or activity as a guest. If not, take a deep breath and dive in. You can always withdraw gracefully if it turns out not to be what you are looking for.*

THE ART OF CONVERSATION

TIP #4:

GET TO KNOW PEOPLE AT YOUR NEW GROUP

So you've joined an organization. You've begun attending meetings or get-togethers, and you've signed up to help with a project. You are evaluating the organization for its "fit" with you, and you are keeping your eyes open for more in-depth participation in the future. You are ready to show your value so that people will want to add you to their networks. What do ninety percent of people do wrong at this point? They hang out with the one person they already know, or they make one new friend at the first meeting and cling to that friend forever after.

I once was asked to make a presentation at a large, office-wide quarterly meeting at my company. In addition to my presentation, awards were being bestowed and the mood was upbeat as people filed into the room and took seats. But, as I watched, I saw that everyone talked to and sat with their peers from the cubicle next to theirs. People from each division stayed with their own immediate colleagues and friends. Even though this was a great time to get to know people from elsewhere in the company, no one seemed to be making the effort. When I got to the podium, I asked people to raise their hands if they were sitting with or talking with someone they didn't already know. **Not one person raised his hand.** What an incredible opportunity gone to waste.

It is everyone's tendency to stick with the familiar. It's excusable, too. You may sit near someone in your day-to-day world but rarely have a chance to catch up with them. Or you may meet someone you like at your first volunteer shift at the Food Bank and want to get to know them better at subsequent events. Those are good things to do. But to build your network you must do *both*. By all means catch up with the person you already know, but also make an effort to talk to someone new. After all, no matter how good you are at what you do, people who see your value from afar cannot add you to their networks if they do not actually *know* you.

At this point, if I'm giving a presentation, someone in the audience invariably raises his or her hand and says, "I'm not outgoing. I don't know what to talk to people about." I hear you, and I feel your pain. Here are some ideas:

- The easiest way to talk to new people is to ask a buddy you already have in your organization to start a conversation with you and a third person that he or she already knows. This works especially well at work. At organizations, some people choose a new group to join simply *because* they already have a buddy there. It's perfectly fine to be up front with your buddy about wanting to meet more people in the organization. After all, you are going to be spending time there and working with those people—of course you want to know them.

    If you don't have a buddy who's been there awhile but you have befriended another newcomer, the two of you can agree to approach new people together and try to get acquainted. Some people find that starting a three-person conversation is less intimidating and takes off the pressure to be a scintillating companion.

- If you are on your own, the next easiest way to talk to a new person is when you and the new person know a third person in common. You may have been told in advance that your brother's business partner is a member of your new classic car group. You and the new person in the sales department may both have worked in the past with Rita in marketing. If so, directly approach the new person and bring up the connection as you introduce yourself.

Sometimes in random discussion you learn, for example, that another attendee went to the same high school as your best friend. Use that to continue the conversation. I once was on a minibus with ten people I hardly knew, driving long stretches of Texas on a week-long business trip, when another bus rider overheard me mention that I had gone to college at Virginia Tech. He asked if I knew his nieces; in a crazy coincidence, at a school of 25,000 students they turned out to have been sorority sisters of mine. That led to an easy conversation and a jump-started friendship.

A caveat, though: If you have even a sneaking suspicion that the person you know in common may not be thought well of by others (the former colleague who got fired for padding his expense account), don't bring him up! The platitude is true: You are judged by the company you keep. I made that mistake once at one of the national conferences I mentioned earlier. I met someone from a major bank who, when she heard I was from Arizona, told me that she had recently been to my state to meet with her company's team there. "Oh, you must know so-and-so!" I exclaimed, looking for common ground. "He's great!" This was met with an awkward silence. In retrospect, I should have realized that the lovable goofball I knew was probably not making a great impression at headquarters.

- If you don't know someone in common and none of your buddies are around, here are some questions to ask to kick off a conversation with a new person after you've introduced yourself.

If you are at a company event and meeting a fellow employee:

"How long have you worked here?"

"What does your area/unit do?"

"Where did you work before you worked at General Products Unlimited?"

If you are at an event for a new organization you've just joined:

Ask about club activities. "What time is the annual picnic next week?" "How do I sign up for a volunteer shift?" "What is the format that committee meetings follow?"

Or ask the person about his experience. "Is this your first event with the Boy Scouts?"

"What other Historical Society events have you been to?"

If the other person is a long-time participant:

"I'm new to the dental association, what do you like about it?"

"What activities do you like best or have found most valuable?"

"What should I make sure to participate in?"

Or, "Can I get your insights on what I should do to make my membership/participation really worthwhile?"

More stock questions:

Depending on the time of year, you can ask "Do you have any summer vacation/Spring Break/Fall Break plans you are looking forward to?" or "Are you taking any time off over Christmas?"

"What other organizations are you involved in?"

"Are you from this area originally?" or, "Did you grow up around here?" If the answer is no, ask "Where did you grow up?" *Do not* ask, however, "What part of town do you live in?" since it can come across as though you are subtly trying to determine their wealth or status.

Some conversation-starting questions may be easier to ask if you first volunteer a little information about yourself:

"Boy, am I looking forward to June when I get my week at the beach. Do you have any good summer plans?"

"I've got to get home and walk the dog. He's a spoiled rotten yellow lab. Do you have pets?"

A good way to ask about outside interests is:

"So what do you do when you're not designing graphic illustrations for Acme Public Relations?"

When the other person answers by telling you that he plays electric guitar in a band on the weekends (following Tip #2 by being interesting and memorable), this gives you the chance to respond by saying that you love guitar, and you yourself have attended twenty-seven Cheap Trick concerts in your lifetime and fly to a different concert city every year to see them perform (now you are memorable, too!).

Here is a last conversational question that, in the right circumstance, is a sure winner. It is not appropriate in every situation, since sometimes you are not entitled to know the answer and can appear intrusive. But as a lobbyist I meet new politicians and elected officials all the time, and this question is the gold standard guaranteed to kick off a lengthy conversation. It also is useful when meeting new people from your own company:

"What are you working on?"

Even if the person launches into a thirty-minute monologue, if you listen politely and enthusiastically, you will have a new friend for life. Plus, you might even learn something new.

Don't be a downer

A note of caution here: *Do not* kick off a conversation, or try to find common ground, with negative comments. The person you are talking to may not agree with statements like "Can you believe how disorganized these volunteers are?" or "Boy, the president sure droned on and on—this meeting could have been half an hour shorter." Not only will these comments make you look like a negative and critical person, you are communicating to the other person that you are the kind of person who may say something like that about *them* some day.

Even if your pessimistic thoughts are about the weather or traffic, you still do not want to create the impression that you are a downer. If people are talking about these common conversational topics, be the person who says something positive, or at least neutral. When everyone else complains about the week of rain, you be the individual who says, "I can't wait 'til the sunny weather returns." This quality will make people gravitate toward you without even realizing it.

Keep it moving

Sometimes, of course, your challenge is not thinking of something to say, but extricating yourself from a conversation that has run its course. As I pointed out at the beginning of this chapter, many people, once they have found a single conversational partner, want to be in it for the long haul; it's so much easier than having to meet another new person! How do you conclude those interactions in a way that leaves a positive impression but allows you to continue to meet other people? The easiest "out" is to announce a need to go elsewhere—the restroom, to make a phone call, or to get something to drink—although this last option may backfire if the other person eagerly replies how thirsty they are and that they will join you. And, if you choose this course, you must actually go where you said you were going. You can also simply say, "I've really enjoyed talking with you. I need to get over and talk to so-and-so, but this has been fun/educational/interesting, and I look forward to working with you on the Boy Scout merit badge committee/annual fundraiser/yearly continuing education seminar."

•••

A really important point about Tip #4: This may feel and sound like we are back to "networking"—trying to get to know more and more people. We are not. You are reaching out to people at an organization you have joined where you have committed to demonstrating value. Now that you have joined this group, you are talking to the people there because you want them to know you and remember you, so that when they see how good you are (back to Tip #1) they will want to add you to their networks.

It may be that the ideas I'm offering here help you become a better conversationalist in many environments—if so, that's great. But when it comes to building your network, this Tip is in service to demonstrating the quality of your work and the value you would add to their networks. You are not just trying to be liked. Hopefully we all like and enjoy talking to a great many people. When it comes to recommending someone for a job or using our own resources and contacts to help someone, however, that value-based subset of individuals is much smaller. Never forget that being liked is no substitute for being a valuable problem-solver in someone's life.

Another point: Many people decide to try to create a network of relationships only when they suddenly need a new job or have to meet a sales goal. That is the time when good relationship-builders rely on the networks they've already built. The purpose of Tip #3 (Join organizations) and Tip #4 (Get to know people) is not to get clients or ask for help in finding a new job. While those may be the ultimate, long-term rewards that you reap from your network one day, you are not demonstrating to someone else the value you could bring to their lives when you have an immediate, apparent objective.

I observe this mistake all the time; it is one of the biggest misconceptions about building a professional relationship network and why I am anti-"networking." "Networking" suggests meeting as many people as possible and telling them about your goals right away, in hopes that one of them will suddenly reply by saying "Really? I'd love to sign up for a year's contract with your company!" That is marketing and sales, not developing meaningful connections. Building relationships is surrounding yourself with friends and colleagues who value you. They offer you support and allow you to call upon them in time of need. They are willing to help you because you provide benefit to their lives.

There is nothing wrong with marketing and sales. When you market, however, you are not building relationships and you are not adding people to your network. You may develop a sales lead that results in an opportunity to pitch your wares in depth, but it *won't* add you to someone's relationship network. That may happen later if you get the business and provide terrific value with the service or product. It's important not to confuse the two.

Last year I was at an event talking with a trusted professional friend named Tim when an acquaintance of his named Jeff approached us and joined the conversation. After a couple of moments of introductory chitchat, Jeff announced that he had been recently laid off from his job. He then described the type of work he was looking for and gave me his card, asking if I would let him know if I heard of anything. I suspect Jeff thought he was "networking," but in reality he was marketing himself. I took his card and wished him well, but I did not feel compelled to share resources or contacts, and I certainly was not in a position to recommend him—I didn't even know him!

Had Jeff been a dedicated practitioner of value-based relationship building, the conversation might have gone very differently. Let's say Jeff had previously forged a deep connection with Tim by demonstrating outstanding work as a leader of their Rotary Club. At the event, upon seeing that Tim knew me, Jeff could have asked Tim if he would be willing to introduce us and recommend my help with Jeff's job search. Even without such a request, having observed Jeff's work at Rotary, Tim would have been much more likely in our conversation to spontaneously chime in with compliments about Jeff. With Tim's endorsement, I would have given serious thought to options and resources for Jeff and offered assistance.

PUTTING IT INTO PRACTICE
TIP #4 – Get to Know People at Your New Group

Past: *Think of the people you've gotten to know most recently. Can you recall how your first conversations started or what you talked about? Who approached whom first?*

Present: *Think of an organization, a work team, or some other group that you are part of **right now** where you don't know every single person there. At your very next meeting or event approach one person you don't know, introduce yourself and begin a short conversation about the group and your mutual involvement in it.*

Future: *Once you have joined a new group as recommended in Tip #3, identify a few people there who seem as though they would be friendly or easy to meet. At your next meeting or activity, make it a goal to approach one of these people with the conversational tactic that feels most comfortable for you. Then, at each successive meeting, approach the next person on your list. Consider a five-minute conversation a win!*

THE INDIVIDUAL CONNECTION

TIP #5:

BUILD RELATIONSHIPS ONE PERSON AT A TIME

Think of relationship building as deliberate friendship building. And friendships happen one person at a time, right? Even if you become friends with several people at the same time—maybe at a new school or a new job—each friendship develops at a different speed because it is based on the unique connection between two individuals. This is true for professional relationships as well. Equating professional relationship building to friendship, however, does not mean that these relationships have to be intense; everyone in your network does not have to be able to sub as best man at your wedding. But your relationship with each member of your network will have its own special qualities. You do not want your network to be just a bunch of people you know.

How would you describe how you became friends with the people who are your pals today? They probably are people with whom you shared experiences over time. Sometimes a friendship germinates from a single formative or important experience, but typically you have racked up the miles, so to speak. We tend to think that our friends are people with whom we have a lot in common, and it may be that we are more likely to connect with people who are similar to ourselves. Still, in many cases the most important component of friendship is simply time spent together.

This is true for developing network relationships as well. As you know by now, I cringe when I see "networking" events advertised in business publications or at chambers of commerce. The idea that you can go to an event at 5 p.m., hand out business cards to a dozen strangers with whom you chat superficially for five minutes, and leave at 7 p.m. having built your network, is laughable. You'd probably never leave a two-hour party and call the people you just met there your friends. In fact, just yesterday a friend of mine who retired and moved to a new city told me that she and her husband had tried exactly that and failed. Despite attending all sorts of social events to meet new people, they had been unable to develop anything beyond acquaintances. I referenced Tip #3 (Find new places to show value) and suggested they get involved in charitable work or become leaders in a club around a hobby that they enjoyed.

View Tip #5 – Build relationships one person at a time – as the fine point on Tip #4 – Get to know people at your new group. Tip #4 says reach out to new people when you attend a club event or join an organization—don't just wait for them to notice how valuable you are and come up to you. Otherwise they may only ever admire you from afar! But without Tip #5 the overeager can misfire, turning Tip #4 back into "networking" artificiality. Tip #5 is the reminder that your goal is to form real relationships, not add names to a roster of "connections."

Therefore, when you reach out to new people at your new organizations, don't take the approach that you have to meet everyone there the first day. Your best balance is to get acquainted with—not just meet—one or two new people and have meaningful interaction with them. Talk about the things that make both them and you interesting. Don't look around the room for other people to talk to or have a goal in your head of meeting a certain number of new people each time (a typical "networking" fallacy). Instead, take a deep breath, slow down and focus on the person in front of you. What are they like? What is important to them? Do you have something in common?

I was initially invited to join the board of directors of my local figure skating club because the club was having legal problems and a friend on the board thought that as a lawyer I could help. I hit it off right away with the board president and, between her and my friend, felt quite welcome from day one. We resolved the legal issues and I continued to volunteer on the board and for the club. When the club's annual skating competition rolled around the following spring, I learned that one of the board's responsibilities was to coordinate a constant stream of home-cooked refreshments throughout the competition weekend. As someone who considers a bowl of cereal to be cooking (it counts because you're adding two ingredients together), I began to panic as potluck assignments were handed out. I enviously watched as another "non-cooking" board member whom I didn't know well was assigned what seemed her usual competition responsibility—purchasing paper plates and plastic cutlery. The president, seeing my fallen expression, suggested that I partner with this woman on the big paper goods buy. The woman seemed less than enthused, but we agreed to meet at Costco in a few days. We had a successful shopping trip, laughing together about our shared ineptitude in the kitchen. It was the beginning of a wonderful professional relationship and friendship. Twenty years later, that fellow non-cook is my "in case of emergency" contact. Yet I served on that board with her for almost a year before we really got to know one another.

Providing value for someone and getting to know them do not always happen simultaneously or even in the same order each time. In the previous example, I had served the skating club for a year before I really got to know my Costco-trip partner. Other times you will not even meet the person you are helping until much later. I once had a co-worker ask me to help a member of his network. Both my co-worker and his friend were Californians but the friend had been assigned by her company to monitor the Utah legislature and needed to hire a lobbyist there. Although I lived in Arizona I had covered Utah state government for several years already, so I was happy to help out my co-worker when his friend called asking for recommendations.

More than six months later I was at an industry conference in Hawaii when another attendee approached me. She introduced herself as the co-worker's friend I had helped with Utah. She told me that the lobbyist she had hired at my recommendation was doing an outstanding job. She was so grateful that, when she heard that I would be attending this conference, she made it a priority to seek me out and thank me in person.

This was a textbook example of someone wanting to add me to their network because of the value I had previously provided them. We spent a fair amount of time together during the conference and parted fast friends. To this day she is a valuable member of my network from whom I've sought aid many times over the years. But I didn't get to know her until long after I had provided her with assistance and demonstrated my own value as a good contact to have.

Here I will emphasize once again that in building strong professional relationships *nothing* is more important than adding value. Your proven delivery of value to others' lives is the single most important reason that they will want you in their network, even if they don't know you very well. Although I had only a single interaction with the hotel concierge and the Accounts Payable employee (in the stories from the first chapter of this book), they both demonstrated such value that I would have been happy to leap to their professional assistance if they had asked. Frequently, however, people experience over time the value you add to their lives. If you are on a committee in your club, or on a project team at work, you will be doing your best work over days, months, or even years. You will create the strongest and most long-lasting relationships if during this time you get to know your colleagues one at a time as individuals. They also are more likely to want to reciprocate and add value to *your* life the better they know you.

PUTTING IT INTO PRACTICE
TIP #5 – Build Relationships One Person at a Time

As we discussed, Tip #5 is the fine point on Tip #4, and putting it into practice will be very similar.

Past: *Think of three "work friends" you have gotten to know in the past. How did you go from becoming just co-workers to becoming work friends? Has a co-worker turned into a friend because of efforts he or she made to get to know* **you** *better?*

Present: *Think of another member of an organization that you are in, or a co-worker who right now you know just well enough to say hello to. The very next time you see or talk to that person, try to get to know them better by taking a few moments to ask them about the work they are doing or about themselves. (If you are not sure what to ask about, refer to suggested topics in Tip #4.)*

Future: *If you followed the "Future" practical advice for Tip #4, you will have approached a couple of new people and started conversations with them. Anticipate the next time you will see those people and commit to yourself that you will engage with each one and spend a few minutes conversing. If it would be helpful, write down what you talked about the first time—it might be the perfect conversation starter the next time around.*

THE ROOKIE MISTAKE

TIP #6:

DON'T FOCUS ONLY ON "IMPORTANT" PEOPLE

We've all done it. We want to meet the important person and shake his or her hand. The celebrity, the congressman, the CEO—we can't wait to bask in the glow for a few moments and later tell the story of the three sentences we exchanged with that person. I'm guilty—I'm still telling people about the one-minute-long conversation I had with presidential candidate Jeb Bush during a 2016 campaign stop in Phoenix. (In my own defense, video of the exchange did wind up on national television, so it's a good story.) For most of us, seeing or meeting a celebrity brightens our life. *People* magazine is a best-seller for a reason.

Too many people, however, when an "important" person is around, miss opportunities to get to know people who can actually be valuable members of their own network. Or, they ignore the chance to deepen the relationships they currently have. Instead of paying attention to the other people present, they are busy scurrying around the room to get near the important person, talking to others distractedly as they keep one eye open for the "big chance."

This is squandering the opportunity to work on your real relationships. First, the reality is that no three-minute or even hour-long conversation with the company president is going to add you to their network, or them to yours. They have too many peers of their own with whom to connect. Unless you are on their level professionally or socially, you just are not equipped to show them enough value during a conversation to pique their interest in you. (Frankly, your greatest chance of becoming part of a VIP's network is to go back to Tip #1 and be good at your job. Smart leaders are always looking for good people to surround themselves with.)

Second, people know when they are receiving only half of your attention during a distracted conversation as you wait for your big moment. If they remember you at all in the future, it is likely to be unfavorably. No one likes to be dismissed by a "climber." People will be less inclined to want to add you to their networks than they were before you had a conversation with them, no matter what kind of value you are exhibiting as the treasurer of the engineering society.

Finally, there is the real risk that you have misidentified who the important person really is. In your haste to get face time with the celebrity of the moment, you may miss gems who could be delightful and valuable members of your network.

When I moved to Arizona, I practiced law with a woman who eventually became the governor of Arizona. At the time I met her, she was a partner at my law firm and not engaged in politics. I worked with her for several months on a major piece of litigation and even attended a concert with her and some friends one night. Years later she became the state attorney general and then was elected governor.

Flash forward ten years. I had just been hired in my new corporate job and was asked by the bigwig regional leader of my company to attend a political event for hundreds of people in a hotel ballroom at which the governor, my former colleague, was the guest speaker. Generously, the Bigwig had invited me to accompany him to the small, VIP-only reception beforehand at which the governor would be shaking hands. We walked into the small salon to see about seventy-five people milling around. Since this was a pricy event, these folks were the bigwigs of their own companies. Right away I recognized the CEO of an important health insurance company and the president of our major league baseball team. On one side of the room, a line of VIPs was queueing to have their photographs taken with the governor. My Bigwig turned to me and said, with a challenge in his voice, "Well, Ellen, you tell me you know the governor. Can you get my picture with her?" At that moment the room lights blinked on and off as a signal that it was time to leave the small reception and head to the great hall for dinner. At the same time, the line of VIPs waiting their turn for a photograph was still at least ten people long. I had two minutes to make good.

"Yes, Steven, I can," I said. And I approached the *photographer*, whom I'd known for years, having first met him at a political event in the mid-90s. He is a nice guy whose true love is volunteering for Habitat for Humanity, but photography pays the bills. I had always greeted him and taken time to chat whenever I saw him, in contrast to typical event attendees for whom he probably was an anonymous background figure. I whispered to him what I needed, and he swung into action. "Governor, just a moment, if you could hold it right there," he said to the governor, and "Sir, just a moment please" to the next VIP in line. Before the line of waiting VIPs knew what was happening, the photographer had placed my

Bigwig into the frame with the governor ahead of everyone else; the flash glared and the photo was done.

The moral of this story is that the important person in any given scenario is not always who you think it is. By trying too hard to be strategic about whom you meet, you can miss out. In this case, no matter how well I knew her, the governor never could have risked offending the waiting line of VIPs by allowing my Bigwig to cut in line ahead of all those other bigwigs. But ever since our kindergarten class picture, we all do what the photographer tells us, right?

A caveat. There is a difference between targeting celebrities and "important" people and targeting "regular" people you want to meet for a specific reason. Sometimes someone in your network is helping you meet a person who could be a lead to a job or other opportunity (more later on this). Or maybe you talk often on the phone with super-competent Denise in the Cash Management department and now would like to meet her in person at the annual corporate holiday party. Think of the story in the last chapter about the person who tracked me down at a conference because I had recommended a lobbyist to her over the phone. Others will be agreeable about helping you find these "regular" folk and will not take offense at your searching the crowd. As I mentioned in discussing Tip #4 (Get to know people at your new group), sometimes your best beginning conversational gambit is mention of a mutual friend. If there is someone around who works at Universal Products with your next-door neighbor, by all means find her and meet her.

The reality is that you do not know when you meet someone whether they will become important in your life. Neither will you know in advance who the people are to whose lives you might add the most value. As you go about your work and your participation in organizations, treat everyone as a potential member of your network. Be conversational and friendly as you engage with people. Follow Tip #4 and reach out, and follow Tip #5 and commit to yourself that you will try to get to know people as individuals. Then make the effort to do so.

PUTTING IT INTO PRACTICE
TIP #6 – Don't Focus Only on "Important" People

Past: *Think of someone you have known in your life who seemed unremarkable at the time, but who later became successful or accomplished. Have you ever known anyone in an ordinary way (a neighbor, someone on the mat next to you at yoga class, an intramural sports teammate, etc.) who you found out later was a VIP? Is there someone you know who lacks star credentials or status, but who has provided invaluable help to you in your professional life?*

Present: *As you put Tips #4 and #5 into practice and approach people in your existing groups whom you don't already know, deliberately choose at least one person who is quiet, hangs back from the group, or does not exude "star power" in any way.*

Future: *Once you've joined a new group and, as suggested under Tip #4, have identified a few people in your new organization whom you would like to get to know, put at least one person on that list who is quiet, hangs back from the group, or does not exude "star power." At an upcoming meeting or activity, make it a goal to approach this person with the conversational tactic that feels most comfortable to you. Then, make sure you have another conversation with them the next time you see them.*

THE SECOND ROOKIE MISTAKE

TIP #7:

DON'T LIMIT YOURSELF TO PEOPLE WHO ARE JUST LIKE YOU

It's human nature to gravitate toward people who are similar to us. In addition to hanging out with people we already know, we tend to hang out with people whose circumstances are like ours. Think of all the young moms huddled in a corner at the neighborhood party comparing notes on second grade teachers. In the professional world we spend time in group settings with the people in our own field, the people at our same career level, and especially the people who are in our age range.

I was helped early in my career by three older gentlemen in their sixties. They were all senior lobbyists at the state capitol where I was on staff. All three were extremely accomplished by the time I met them and had had illustrious careers. One even went on to be a United States ambassador—an achievement resulting from his extraordinary value to his own impressive network, no doubt. These successful men had no need to take interest in a young senate employee.

I worked with them in my staff role, however, and my good work impressed them. (I cannot say it often enough: It's all about Tip #1 – Be good at your job.) As a result, each of these men took it upon himself to recommend me for a prestigious association CEO job, despite the well-known fact that the leading candidate for the position was the sitting Arizona Speaker of the House. In the face of this standout competition, at age thirty-two I was selected to become one of the youngest CEOs of a state bankers association in the country. Even more notably, I was only the fourth woman nationwide to ever serve in the top role at a state trade association for what was then an industry dominated by male leaders. My salary doubled, and my achievement was extraordinary enough to be noted on the front page of the business section of the state's largest newspaper. Despite my abilities and qualifications, however, this never would have happened had these three accomplished men not taken an interest in me. I was unimportant and unnecessary to their careers and professional success. Had they not been men who found value in connecting with people at all stages of their careers, I never even would have been considered for that job.

Even though I have benefited dramatically from older people reaching out to a younger me, I personally struggle with this Tip the most. Although I have always related well to people who are older than I am, I tend to be skeptical of young people in general. I could have invented the catch-phrase from the '60s: Don't trust anyone under thirty. Worse, as the years go by, I fight a tendency to revise that number upward. But because of the incredible importance of this Tip, I make a conscious effort to relate to and learn from people my junior. Not only has it been rewarding beyond my expectations, but these connections help me to remain up to speed on social trends in today's professional world. If I can get outside my comfort zone and relate well to people who are unlike me, so can you.

One of the most "big deal" members of my network and a close friend is someone I originally met only because another member of my network asked me to help him. One day during a time I was serving on a chamber of commerce board of directors, the young lady who was the chamber's media director came to me and asked if I would meet with her husband. He had just graduated from law school and was unhappy with his current job practicing law in a firm. He was hoping to change career paths and was seeking advice. Because of my natural skepticism about young people, I only reluctantly agreed to her request. Frankly, the fact that she herself was highly competent tipped the scales—she was a valuable member of my network and I wanted to continue a good relationship with her. Once I agreed to the meeting, however, I procrastinated, putting it off as long as possible. Eight months after her initial request I finally was cornered into having lunch with her husband. (This part of the story should not be used as relationship building guidance, by the way. Nobody's perfect.)

To my surprise, we clicked at lunch and became friends. He was impressive, and I could tell he was smart and capable. I became a regular career advisor to this young man. Several years later he was named to a top position on our governor's staff. After five years in that role he moved to multiple prestigious private-sector jobs, all while being wooed for high-level staff positions by major figures on the national political stage. He remains in the governor's inner circle. I am lucky to count him as one of my closest personal friends—and it all started with the lunch that I had been so reluctant to schedule.

In another example, our legislature employs college seniors from our state universities as interns during the legislative session. These kids are given significant levels of responsibility at our otherwise understaffed capitol. I am always friendly to these interns and offer help where I can. Last year I acquired a client because our governor's chief attorney wrote a letter to the client recommending me. This attorney, who is almost fifteen years younger than I am, likes to tell people that I was the first person to be nice to him when he arrived on the capitol scene more than twenty years ago as a college intern. No one then knew he would go on to excel in law school, clerk for a state supreme court justice, and become the general counsel to the governor. Since then he has received a presidential appointment as a federal judge. All I knew back then was that he worked earnestly and diligently, and I was impressed.

In both of these situations I offered the value of my friendliness and professional experience to these young men who were just starting to make their way. Had I been thinking instead about what value these untested youngsters could bring to me, these relationships would never have gotten off the ground.

A conservative Republican friend recently shared an interesting story of being invited to a dinner with some prestigious public figures. As he and his wife were being led to their seats, he noted with disappointment that they were passing the tables where the Republican leaders he most wanted to meet were sitting. His heart sank further when he arrived at the table and saw that a noted liberal Democrat was their host. My friend kept his disappointment to himself, of course, and sat down to make the best of dinner. He told me that as the evening went on, he discovered that their Democrat companion was the most gracious person at the entire event. In addition to being kind and welcoming, she was the only host who took time to give her table guests a tour of the historic building where the dinner was being held. My friend told me he felt very lucky to have met this leader, whom he might never have gotten to know had he been seated at the Republican table of his choice.

There are two points to be learned here. First, making an effort to build relationships with people different from you can expand your network significantly. Most people surround themselves with other people just like them. If you follow this Tip, however, you will be broadening your relationship-building efforts to connect with different kinds of people. You will then have a potential connection to all of the people in *their* networks who are dissimilar to you and whom you would be unlikely to ever get to know were it not for your relationship with their friend.

Second, in today's world most people exist in an echo chamber of news and social media that reinforces their existing opinions and beliefs. There is a lamentable lack of respect for different viewpoints and a lack of kindness toward those who have them. Leadership gurus will tell you, however, that one of the traits of successful people is that they actively seek out perspectives that differ from their own. If you are gracious and respectful toward people who are unlike you and appear interested in forging relationships with them, you will stand out from the crowd. Our core relationship-building principle will be at work here, as you will once again be demonstrating the value that you can add to another person's network—that of respectfully offering a unique and therefore prized point of view.

Bottom line: Admit your preexisting biases and consciously set them aside. Don't let them impede your development of value-based relationships for your network.

PUTTING IT INTO PRACTICE
TIP #7 – Don't Limit Yourself to People Who Are Just Like You

Past: *Think of people different from you who are important in your life. Is there someone much older than you—maybe a teacher, or an older colleague who has helped you in your professional life? Have you helped a person with whom you have nothing in common? Perhaps you have a close friend whose political views are so different from yours that you think they are crazy—but you're pals anyway.*

Present: *As you put Tips #4 and #5 into practice and approach people in your existing world whom you don't already know, deliberately choose at least one person who seems very different from you.*

Future: *Once you've joined a new group and, as suggested in Tip #4, have identified a few people there whom you would like to get to know, put at least one person on that list who seems very different from you. At an upcoming meeting or activity, make it a goal to approach this person with the conversational tactic that feels most comfortable to you. Then, make sure you have another conversation with them the next time you see them.*

DEEPENING THE RELATIONSHIP

TIP #8:

FOLLOW UP

You've joined the organizations and expanded your reach at work. You are working hard to be a problem solver and someone whom others find capable and effective. You are meeting people to whom you can demonstrate your value. What happens next? What can you do to help these meetings and positive interactions become relationships?

Unless you follow up, the great conversation you had at the quarterly results meeting or during your volunteer shift at the homeless shelter will be just that—a great conversation. It will not magically turn itself into a great relationship. Even if you are guaranteed to see the person in a month at the next board or committee meeting and will be able to talk again then, following up will help move your new relationship forward and cement you in the person's mind.

Relationships are built in small steps, especially for adults. I look back fondly on school, when you could hang out for hours with people and become friends effortlessly. Now, even in the workplace with people you see daily, time is peskily taken up by actual work. This is why working together on a project or in a club accelerates professional friendships. Not only are you demonstrating value, you are spending time together, which creates a bond. For those to whom you've demonstrated value but have yet to get to know, however, relationships are built in increments. You talk to someone for five minutes today, then another five minutes in a couple weeks, then you have coffee two weeks after that, then you greet each other as old friends at the committee meeting a month after that. How do you make those increments happen? By following up.

First, in order to follow up, you need to remember what you talked about in the conversation that you are following up on. In this era of digital record storage, many people no longer bother with business cards. I always collect cards, however, and then write down on the back what I talked about with that person. The card itself is a visual reminder, plus the mere act of writing helps me remember. If I know I'm going to see the person again it's a simple thing to quickly check the back of the card the morning before I attend the meeting or event where they will be present. Of course, you also can take notes digitally.

Any time I've started a new job and consequently been introduced to a lot of people in a short time period, I have created a running alphabetical list of the new people as I met them and included a couple sentences about each. For the first few months I review this document a few times a week as a helpful way to jog my memory. My co-workers have always been surprised and pleased when, as a result of this practice, I greet them by name or remember what they are working on.

I worked with a new photographer recently whose manner and way of working I admired, so at the close of the session I asked him for a card. He did not have any with him, so in a modern-day tech move he "air dropped" his contact information from his cell phone into mine. Did he accomplish the objective of sharing his contact information? Yes. Will it work the same way to jog my memory for follow-up? I'm pretty diligent, so probably yes. In case you are meeting someone less committed to follow-up than I am, however, you should always have *your* business cards handy to give to someone who asks. Why not provide them with the opportunity to be reminded about you the next time they go through their wallet, purse, or briefcase?

Make it a practice to send emails and thank you notes to people you have met and want to get to know better. I try to do this all at once at the end of each week—Friday afternoons are often a good time to find a half hour or hour for this. I pull out the business cards I collected and look at the notes I made on them. Then I go through my calendar for the week and remind myself who I met with, where I went and who I talked to there, and what we talked about. Most of these folks receive a short email from me. I also make sure that I've followed through on any promised actions. Did I share the orthopedic surgeon referral with the guy in human resources? Did I email the article on autonomous vehicles to the techie who is on the trash pickup committee with me?

When I offer this advice, people often complain that they don't know what to say in an email. Three or four sentences are enough. Here are some suggestions:

- I generally write how much I enjoyed meeting the person and then I reference the conversation we had—classic cars, or the new project in Underwriting, or our mutual love of corn on the cob. It doesn't matter what it is, as long as it shows that the conversation made an impression on you.

- If I can, I tell them how much I appreciated learning something from them. There is not a single person on this planet who doesn't like to hear that. Be sincere, though. I once, out of general enthusiasm, said to a retiring colleague, "I've learned so much from you!" She responded, "Like what?" Long pause... lesson learned. Don't say it if you can't elaborate when asked.

- I usually close by saying I hope to see them at the next club meeting or school board event. You do not have to be witty or have Pulitzer Prize-worthy writing skills—the fact that you're following up is what matters.

I realize there are generational differences in methods of preferred electronic communication. Gen Y and Z members may prefer texting, social media, or the latest smartphone mind meld that has been developed in the time it has taken me to type this sentence. For electronic communication, however, I strongly urge email. First, most of you reading this book are hoping to build a professional network. Email, at least at this point in time, remains the preferred method of communication in the office workplace. Second, an email message remains present and visible in an email inbox and can be revisited or more easily responded to—if the recipient is so inclined—days or weeks after its initial receipt. Finally, email is the easiest format for intelligent, abbreviation-free sentences, which are your best bet for making a positive impression in the early stages of a relationship. (In other words, no matter how much you want to sign off with TTYL, don't do it.)

Follow-up is not just for building relationships; it is a lodestar of maintaining them. Send emails when you encounter people you haven't seen in a while, or thank-you emails if they've provided you with assistance.

If someone has really helped you, instead of an email send a handwritten note, or even a gift.

Once when I was promoted at my old company, the new job came with a slew of additional retirement benefits that were wonderful but complicated to understand. A kind executive in our out-of-state HR department spent forty-five minutes with me on the phone explaining the ins and outs, even though there was a written manual on the subject I could have consulted. The day after our conversation, I hand-wrote and mailed him a thank-you note. Years later after he had left the company, I ran into him again by sheer coincidence. The first words out of his mouth were, "I still have the thank-you note you sent me. It meant so much to me!"

Recently I helped a close and important member of my network with a professional crisis that he encountered. After a few tense weeks, everything was resolved favorably. Shortly thereafter, I was touched to receive a book from him about hiking (thanks to my adherence to Tip #2, he knows that hiking is one of my interests), accompanied by a heartfelt thank-you card. I loved the book, the card, and the feeling of being appreciated for the help I had given.

Frankly, good manners are in such short supply these days that people are appreciative of *any* acknowledgement of assistance. My financial advisor once gave me four front-row tickets for a Major League Baseball game (to which I immediately invited three chamber of commerce friends, thus nurturing my own network). During the game I asked a nearby fan to take a photo of us in front of the field, which I texted to my advisor, saying thank you. (In this case a text was a meaningful follow-up that could make the most impact, since it allowed to me to share the photo in real time and let him see the fun I was having thanks to him.) The next time I saw him, he told me how much he appreciated my text. He said he rarely ever received thanks or acknowledgement from recipients of his baseball-ticket largesse. He ended the conversation by saying he would get me tickets to *two* games the following year.

Another way to follow up with a new acquaintance or to keep in touch with an existing network member is to send articles about topics of mutual interest. You also can send notes when the person is in the news. In the "old days" articles were clipped out of the newspaper and sent by snail mail, but today they can be sent digitally via links in an email. (If someone is featured prominently in an article, however, the actual print copy is often very welcome. When I was on the front page of the newspaper's business section, I appreciated all the folded newspaper clippings I received in the mail, and so did my grandmother.)

If a member of your network lives somewhere else and their city or region is in the news, send a note: "Saw the tornados in the news, hope you and your family are ok!" If a colleague or acquaintance says something positive about someone in your network that you haven't seen in a while, it's a prime opportunity to send a short email letting the person know that their name came up: "I hope your ears were burning today. Bob and I were talking about how we couldn't have completed the zoning project last year without you." A note congratulating someone on her ten-year anniversary with the company or a link to an article about elephants to someone who volunteers at the zoo are other nice ways to create a connect point. It also says that they are interesting enough that you thought of them when the topic came up again, and who doesn't like to hear that? I still treasure the magazine article about Africa from *The Economist* mailed to me by the then-governor of Colorado with the handwritten comment, "Thought you'd enjoy this. –Bill," after I sat next to him at a dinner one evening and discussed international travel. If the governor of Colorado can find time to do this, so can you.

By the way, I know it is tempting to use the shortcuts offered by social media to do your follow-up. It's so easy to write a comment on LinkedIn or Facebook in response to the post about the job promotion or the award received. After all, your total investment of time equals ten seconds. But the recipient of those comments *knows* that it took you ten seconds. You do not stand out in any way from the other fifty people who also responded to the post. A separate email or note, however, does make you shine.

A side note here on social media for network building. I agree with the experts who say you must be on LinkedIn if you are looking for a job. Today it functions as a database of professionals and their qualifications. I read recently that fifty-seven percent of Human Resource professionals won't even interview someone unless the person has a profile on LinkedIn. Having said that, however, I do not find social media effective as a true network-building tool. Instead, it is a marketing tool that provides a large audience to which you can advertise yourself. That may be a benefit in your line of work—I enjoy following people on LinkedIn, for example, who post interesting commentary in their fields. LinkedIn also alerts me to people who advertise themselves as having specific skills or subject matter expertise.

But, the network you truly want is one of people who have actually experienced your value. Those people will want to support you, and they will be there for you in time of need because you are valuable to them. That kind of network happens via the Tips I am describing in this book, not with computer clicks or article posting. When a significant issue arises in your life, while you can send an online message asking your social media connections for help, in all likelihood the ones who will answer your call for assistance are the ones who are in your real, value-based network. Do not confuse knowing a lot of people, via social media or any other means, with having a large network. A small network of people who truly find you valuable will be more rewarding in the long run than a lengthy contacts list of people with whom you are acquainted.

Social media used as an avenue for one-on-one, individualized connection can be effective follow-up though. Once at lunch a long-time member of my network revealed that she had owned St. Bernard dogs as a child. She told me several stories about her love for these pets, but when I asked if she had one now she shook her head sadly and told me that the weather in Phoenix where we live is just too hot for them.

Several months later on vacation I found myself at an unplanned stop at the Bernard Pass in Switzerland, where these dogs are bred and trained. I took a photo of the cutest one and posted it on Facebook with the caption, "This one's for you, Kelly!" She replied with the comment that I had made her day. I'm sure she felt great that in the midst of my trip I had remembered our conversation and singled her out for communication; I know I would have. Generally though, while there's nothing wrong with social media commenting, if you want to make a real impact and build a relationship, take the time to write an email or handwritten note.

Because so many people are on social media, however, it can be a way to stay on the radar of the people in your network, especially those you don't see very often. LinkedIn, with its professional orientation, can be useful for this. You are not building relationships with your LinkedIn postings, but you are alerting your network to your accomplishments and successive job moves. News of your achievements will confirm for them their original assessment that you are a person of value worth including in their networks.

There are many pitfalls with social media platforms, however. Political posts, complaints, too much information about your personal life or struggles—all of these can create negative impressions among people you are hoping to add to your network. Think carefully before you allow someone unfettered access to your personal life. Also realize that people who don't know you well will draw broad conclusions about you from a speck of information. An Instagram post of a margarita on vacation could say "alcoholic" to a nondrinker you just met while working together on the church committee, for example. A Facebook rant about the lousy customer service at Joe's Auto Body Shop could easily be viewed as anger management issues. Right or wrong, it is human nature to make these judgments. At the very least, wait to allow someone into your social media space until after they appreciate your value and know you better; that way your posts and content won't create the entirety of their conception of you.

Back to following up. As I've mentioned previously, you do not know at the time you meet someone whether he or she will become part of your network. Consequently, it is worth following up with anyone you interact with for more than just a few minutes. I can't say it enough: The means by which you will build your network is showing value to others so that they want to add you to their own networks. They must actually know you, however, in order to do so. Follow-up helps them get to know and remember you. Your opportunity to show value may come later, but following up after the first and subsequent interactions begins building that professional friendship. In addition, following up is generally considered a virtue; while it's not enough in itself to create the kind of value necessary for a long-term, supportive relationship, it will reflect well on you. Frankly, many of the people with whom I follow up do not become members of my network. That's okay; following up is a small investment of time for potentially great rewards down the road.

When you follow up after meeting someone what you are really saying is, *I think you are worth getting to know better, which is why I took the time to send this note.* Most of us find it heartwarming to be on the receiving end of this message. After all, it is a sad truth that it's not every day someone paid enough attention to what we were saying to be able to remember it afterwards. People who follow up with meaningful thanks after receiving assistance inspire even more positive feelings. They also make the other person receptive to the possibility that they will add value to their life and become a member of their network. If you hope eventually to be able to turn to your network for help, consider it from their perspective: It's human nature to enjoy helping others who are appreciative of us and our generosity. I'm still smiling about the hiking book my friend sent me.

PUTTING IT INTO PRACTICE
TIP #8 – Follow Up

Past: *Think of someone you know who always follows up. They are great at sending the card, replying to the email, texting you the recommendation for the carpet installer that they promised you when you stopped to chat in the hall at work. Recall times you have followed up—sent a thank you note, a sympathy card, an email to let someone know a project was ongoing, etc.*

Present: *Look back on the past week. Go over in your mind everyone you spoke with for any length of time and what you talked about. Did you meet someone new? Was anyone helpful to you with information or on a project? Did someone give you a gift? Did you really enjoy a conversation with someone that took place during a work interaction? If so, send a follow-up email to that person. Tell them it was nice to meet them, thank them for the help or the gift, or say it was great to catch up. If you agreed to do something for someone and haven't gotten to it yet, do it now.*

Future: *Calendar a half hour at the end of each week to follow up with at least two people with whom you interacted that week. If you said you'd do something for someone and haven't done it, do it during this time. For others, send a short email to each, unless something "bigger" such as a handwritten note, card, or gift is warranted.*

THE BIG TURN-OFF

TIP #9:

BE APPROPRIATE IN YOUR FOLLOW-UP

Dictionary.com defines the word *appropriate* as "suitable or proper in the circumstances." Appropriateness is critical in your follow-up! I am amazed at the number of people who ask for too much, too soon—it's one of the biggest mistakes in trying to build a successful network. After a first conversation or introduction, these people ask for huge favors—hire my nephew, buy the $90,000 computer software that I am selling, introduce me to your uncle the movie producer. I want to shake these people and tell them they are dooming their future with these new potential connections. Even if the request or favor is somehow granted—and many of us are so taken aback in the face of such audacity that we cannot respond truthfully with our real reaction and instead mutter, "I'll see what I can do"—does anyone really feel warmly toward the asker? Under these circumstances the ask-ee feels uncomfortable and taken advantage of. That's not a way to build a long-term relationship.

Remember the college sports support organization that I regretted joining because of the relentless sales tactics of the other members? After my very first club activity, two members called to ask if I would set up sales meetings for them with senior executives at my company. I barely knew these two men; in fact, I even initially confused one of them with another person I also had met the same day. I might have viewed these requests favorably if, after time, I had been impressed by their work for the club. After meeting them only once, however, their requests felt intrusive and put me in the awkward position of having to turn them down or make excuses. As you can imagine, I did not feel warmly toward my new colleagues; instead, I tried to avoid them at successive club events. They inappropriately pushed too hard too soon.

I once was featured in a local magazine article about successful businesswomen. A young woman whom I had never met read the article, looked up my company telephone number and called me out of the blue. When I answered the phone, she told me she had read the article and was calling to ask me to be her mentor. Now, mentoring is a role that, when done right, takes a significant amount of time and effort, so this woman was asking for a substantial commitment from someone she didn't even know. Furthermore, when I asked her what particular career goal she was trying to achieve, she was unable to articulate anything concrete I could help her with. Instead she answered, "Something important and glamorous."

I suspect this person thought she was boldly taking charge of her career. Her request, however, made me very uncomfortable. I was either going to feel bad about saying no, or agree to devote valuable time and attention to someone I had never met, who didn't know what she wanted, and whose professional judgment I was already skeptical about after five minutes of conversation. I did not want to add her to my network; I wanted to get off the phone as quickly as possible.

This young woman would have done better to request a brief telephone or in-person meeting to seek my advice on a single, well-thought-out question. Asking for a full-fledged mentorship relationship right out of the box was off-putting for *any* kind of future interaction. If she had taken a moment to think about the perspective of a person featured in a magazine because of her professional success, she might have guessed that I already would be mentoring others and would be extremely busy. Had she acknowledged this while politely requesting a short meeting at a time and place of maximum convenience for me, I would have been much more receptive to getting acquainted.

Of course, cold calls still have a low chance of success from a network-building standpoint. It is extremely difficult in a brief conversation or get-together to demonstrate value to someone you have never met before. This is the reason short conversations at "networking" events don't result in valuable relationships, and why this chapter is about "follow-up"—the implication here is that there are previous interactions at work or at an organization to follow up *on*.

Nonetheless, if the young woman was determined to try to meet me and had no member of her own network who could introduce us, a request for a short meeting or call would have been the most appropriate way of reaching out: "I know you must be extremely busy, but I would be so grateful for twenty minutes of your time to hear your insights on achieving success…." As I mentioned, it is very difficult to demonstrate value in a short meeting. Therefore this would have been unlikely to add me to her network. But, this approach would not have inspired the negative reaction that her original method did. Also, if I then granted her request for a brief interaction and she conducted herself well in the meeting, I would have been more open to subsequent contact. It would have been a long shot, but I might even have been impressed enough during our meeting to identify her as an intelligent up-and-comer whom I wanted to add to my own network, helping her without her having to ask. This young lady, however, torpedoed any chance she had of building a relationship when she asked for too much too soon. I turned her down because she was inappropriate.

Appropriateness, not only in your follow-up but in the relationship as a whole, is *critical*. Being appropriate is often barely noticeable, but being *inappropriate* is like a warning siren. It repels potential network members like kryptonite. Even with high-quality job performance and a record of problem solving, no one will consider you for their network if you make them feel uncomfortable or as though they are being courted for friendship only because of the benefit they can bring to you. Neither does anyone feel warmly toward those who waste their time or are insensitive to their obligations.

Appropriate follow-up is all about recognizing what the *other* person will positively respond to or appreciate. It also means avoiding doing things that cause someone to experience unpleasant feelings. The young lady who wanted me to be her mentor left me feeling guilty about not helping her, even though her request was misplaced and intrusive. Don't leave bad feelings in your wake by being inappropriate.

As I recommended in Tip #8 (Follow up), it's almost impossible to be inappropriate with a follow-up email or handwritten note. It is the optimal contact after an initial conversation or introduction. It is warm and friendly but requires nothing of the recipient. Then, as you see and talk with a potential network member more often through work or at your organization activities, as long as you are demonstrating value, the relationship will deepen naturally. You will reach a point in your burgeoning relationship with this person where an invitation to get together feels appropriate. What to do at this point? The next step is to suggest getting together for coffee.

The Coffee Invitation

With your coffee invitation you still must keep your relationship development on track, and that means continuing to be appropriate. The first way to do that is to set a time limit in your invitation and keep to it when you meet. If you have invited someone for a twenty-minute coffee, do not, now that you have them in your clutches, hold onto them with a death grip for forty-five minutes, an hour, an hour and a half! You may be with someone who is not comfortable assertively ending meetings, but never fear: A person who feels trapped by you once will never again risk that unpleasant experience. On the other hand, you will make an incredibly positive impression on your guest—and they'd better be your guest, so make sure *you* pick up the check—when at the appointed twenty-minute mark you say something along the lines of "Well, this has been tremendously enjoyable/educational/interesting, but I see that our twenty minutes have flown by and I'm sure you have a busy rest of your day ahead." If the meeting is going well the other person can easily respond that they have more time and would like to continue the conversation. If they are ready to wrap it up, they will appreciate your keeping them on schedule and will be impressed by your understanding of their needs.

Second, remember that at this coffee you are building a relationship, not marketing yourself or your product. Therefore, to deepen your relationship and build your network, **do not ask for anything during your coffee date**. Imagine the situation from the other person's perspective: He or she is very busy and past experience may lead them to suspect that if they are being invited for coffee by someone they don't know well, that person is likely to want something from them. What a pleasant surprise when coffee turns out to be time for getting to know one another and nothing else. And think how much *you* will enjoy the time as well.

It is a universal truth that everyone wants to be understood, yet most people are busy thinking about themselves instead of trying to understand others. But you don't have to garner in-depth insight into someone else's personality or conduct psychoanalysis to understand where they're coming from. Simply reflecting on a few basic principles goes a long way:

- everyone likes to be appreciated;

- no one likes their time wasted;

- everyone in this fast-paced world has too much to do in too little time, and

- everyone has priorities and challenges in their life that don't involve you.

Your consideration of someone else's viewpoint on these elementary concepts will exhibit a rare trait, confirming for them their good judgment in adding you to their network.

Some of you might assume that if coffee is good, lunch is great. So what about the time-honored practice of going to lunch with someone to get to know them better? Proceed with caution; lunch has its pitfalls. Lunch is used so often these days as a marketing tool that its value as a relationship-building tool has been compromised. Many people have become wary of lunch invitations from individuals they hardly know.

People selling something often ask for lunch—a whole hour or more with a captive audience while they tout their product or idea. That's great if the up-front purpose of lunch is a sales discussion. You, however, are trying to build a relationship.

Once again, pause and look at it from the other person's perspective. If he is an Important Person, he has plenty of other Important People to have lunch with and plenty of mandatory business lunches with which to fill up his weeks. He is not wondering what the heck to do every day come noon. Nor are Important People moved by your offer to buy them lunch— they generally have enough people already buying them lunch, or make enough money to buy their own meals, that this is not an enticement.

If you are getting to know an Important Person and want to have lunch with her, ask yourself before you invite her, what is in it for her? Will she enjoy it? Will she gain a benefit from spending time with me? You may have to admit to yourself that the answer is *no*. No shame in that; it does not mean that this won't change in the future as your relationship develops. If the other person is not an Important Person, however, but is of similar stature to you, lunch can be mutually beneficial, and the answers to the above questions can be *yes* for both of you.

Nonetheless, I find the best practice is to reserve lunch for established members of one's network, rather than employing it as a get-to-know-you-better tool. For people you are trying to get to know, an invitation to coffee is more likely to be well-received and cast a more favorable light upon you as the asker. If that goes well and the relationship is deepening, then lunch can come later.

By the way, some of you reading this may have a tendency to evaluate the questions above based on your level of self-confidence—not just pre-lunch but before any meeting or conversation. Remember, though, you are following up on a developing relationship because you are showing value to this person by the quality of your work. Maybe you have solved problems for them in their job, or you are an indispensable member of the real estate agent association philanthropy committee. This means that a likelihood already exists that they want to get to know *you* better and add *you* to their network. The above questions are not an invitation to self-assess your personal charm; they just offer a realistic evaluation of how beneficial the other person would find it to have lunch with you. Start with an invitation to coffee, however, and you are unlikely to go wrong.

• • •

Being appropriate is not only a critical component of creating a network, it is essential to maintaining it successfully. Once you have built a successful professional network, any time you call upon someone in it you must be sensitive to the nature and depth of the relationship. In other words, any request you make of your network friends must "fit." Just as you would not ask a casual business acquaintance to be the godparent of your child, you must think objectively about whether you are close enough to a person in your network for the help you are seeking to not seem out of line. As always, consider the other person's situation and needs. What is the "bigger picture" for this person beyond little old you? Are they swamped with work, or in the middle of their own personal or professional trauma or transition? Are you one of ten or more similar requests they get in a given week?

My friend Sandy is a lobbyist for a major airline. She constantly fields requests for free plane tickets from those in her network having personal emergencies. No matter how close she and I are, I would never consider approaching her on that subject. Putting myself in her shoes, I can see how fatiguing it would be to deal with frantic people who can't see beyond their individual crisis to understand how inappropriate it is to expect her to give away her company's product.

A Safer Approach to Making the Ask

I arrived at a physical therapy appointment the other day in time to overhear the previous patient ask the therapist, "Do you still have that client who is a concert promoter? Will you ask him to get me tickets to the Eagles concert? I need four." I cringed. I could read the visible discomfort written on the therapist's face. She said, "I'll ask him," but I could see that she was not happy about the request, and I wondered if she really would.

The appropriate approach would have been to phrase the request in a less demanding and direct fashion. The patient could have said instead, "Do you still have that client who is a concert promoter? Would you mind asking him if he has any suggestions or recommendations as to where I can track down four tickets to the Eagles? The show is sold out, but I'm dying to go." **Requesting information is a no-fail way to seek assistance from your network.** It offends almost no one, but still makes the ultimate goal clear—this person is looking for tickets, just as someone who requests an informational interview is looking for a job. The physical therapist can ask her concert promoter client for information without feeling as though she is pressuring him. If the concert promoter is feeling generous, this query still lets him respond by offering the four tickets. If he's not, he can offer suggestions as to where to find tickets. No one has to feel uncomfortable.

Everyone's relationships continue unharmed and possibly strengthened from feeling good about helping.

This approach doesn't place the physical therapist in the awkward position of making a big "ask" of her concert promoter client (who probably is begged on a daily basis for sold-out concert tickets). In addition, it allows the physical therapist to choose whether to use her network for someone else's benefit. What if she is planning to call upon this relationship herself in the near future? If the therapist wants to see the Rolling Stones next month, will she really feel no hesitation in asking her client about more free concert tickets?

Requesting information is a great way to approach members of your network when you are looking for *anything*. For the less bold among us this should be a welcome relief, but it is true for everyone.

"I heard there is a job opening at such-and-such company where you used to work. Would you be able to find out anything about it that you can share with me?"

"Can you tell me who I should talk to at your company about contracting with my firm as the supplier of their widgets for the upcoming year?"

Here is the beauty of a value-based network: Your network friends have seen your value and they think you are terrific—that's why you are in their networks and they are in yours. As a result, when asked for information, they often will choose to "go the extra mile" upon hearing your request. Instead of quickly firing off an internal email query about the job opening, they will call HR and tell them you are fabulous and should be hired. Instead of merely forwarding you the link from the company's website about its purchasing processes, they will tell the director of procurement that you are great and would be a reliable company partner for widget production.

On the other hand, if you are asking for help from someone you hardly know and who has not had the opportunity to learn that you are terrific, they might be willing to get you information but will not do anything to get you the position or the contract. If you ask them for these things directly you will only make them uncomfortable. People will put themselves on the line for you only if they think you are worth it. An information request allows people to view you favorably and choose their response on their own.

A final thought on this subject: If the people you are asking for information do not think you are terrific, you need to revisit the earlier Tips in this book.

Using Your Network Appropriately

At one point in my life I thought that I would like to make a career change and become a law professor. I told different lawyer friends in my network about this objective and asked if they had any suggestions (an appropriate information request) as to how to proceed toward this goal. One of them offered to introduce me to a law professor friend who taught at our city's nationally recognized law school. My friend arranged lunch for the three of us (lunch was her suggestion, not mine) during which the professor was quite discouraging about my chances. She indicated that to get any teaching job at all I would have to be willing to move anywhere in the country and would be lucky to get even the lowliest position. I would have to teach for years before being able to work where I liked. She herself had spent a decade as a law school instructor in Arkansas and had only recently been able to return home to Arizona to teach.

This was disheartening. I like Phoenix and I didn't want to move. I wanted to start teaching at the Arizona law school right away. I knew that many law schools often invite law practitioners to teach occasional classes in their areas of specialty, so I decided to aim for that instead, thinking that I could perhaps parlay such a position into an eventual full-time teaching gig.

Recently the school had hired a new dean. She had previously taught in Washington D.C. at a law school near the one I went to. Law schools in our nation's capital often include legislative coursework among their elective options, and I had taken such a class during school. I was sure her D.C. school had offered those options as well. I decided to try to meet her and use that commonality to persuade her that she should hire me to teach a class on legislation, the subject of my "day job."

Before I continue the story, note that I was already following Tip #1 – Be good at your job. I had achieved sufficient academic credentials and professional success to be reasonably qualified to teach a class on this subject at the law school. Had I not, this would have been a futile and ludicrous effort.

One of the lawyer friends whom I had asked for information was an alumna of the local law school. I told her about my idea and asked if she had any information about the school's new leader. In response, my friend invited me to join her at a meet-the-new-dean reception for alumni. I went with her, and in the fleeting two-minute conversation I had with the dean, I mentioned our shared history at D.C. law schools. I added that I had always thought the local law school should follow the D.C. model and offer a class in legislative work. **Instead of talking about my own interest, I pointed out how this could add value to the law school and therefore to the dean.** The state's competing law school had recently received a $100 million bequest from a former student to fund a plethora of new programs. It wasn't a stretch to guess that the new dean would be under pressure to come up with new programs at her school as well, to remain competitive for the state's best students. Therefore I suggested that, since her school was located in the state capital while the other one was not, an entire program related to legislative and government law, with state agency internships, would be something that the other law school in a different part of the state could not do, no matter how much money it had. At no point in the conversation did I mention how I wanted to be a law professor or teach a class.

The dean responded by saying, "What a good idea." That was it. I did not push further, I did not suggest that I be hired to teach this class, I did not monopolize her time at the reception trying to "sell" myself. The next day I mailed her a handwritten note reiterating our shared experience with D.C. schools. I repeated my suggestion that she add a legislative class to the school's curriculum and added a sentence about how, if she ever did so, I would love to teach it. I closed by wishing her well with her new deanship.

By putting my own wish in writing I did not put her in the uncomfortable position of having to come up with an immediate response. Remember, being appropriate and NOT making someone else uncomfortable is key to having them even consider you as a potential member of their network. Not putting the dean on the spot made me more appealing as a professional contact. If, when we were introduced, I had instead said some version of "It's nice to meet you, here's what I want...," her likely reaction would have been a big figurative step back. A written note, however, put absolutely no pressure on her.

Then, in a serendipitous coincidence a few weeks later, I was in the Salt Lake City airport at my gate waiting for my flight home and there was the dean, in the same gate area. I approached her, reintroduced myself, and we chatted for a few moments about our respective visits to Salt Lake City. I was there for a figure skating competition and she was there to watch a collegiate swim meet (both of us clearly following Tip #2 and being interesting). Our discovery of a shared interest in individual competitive sports made it a fun and friendly conversation. We spoke for about ten minutes, in closing I mentioned briefly my interest in teaching a legislative class, and then... *I went back to my original seat and left her alone.* I could easily have glommed on to her, moving to sit by her in the waiting area, or, since we were flying Southwest Airlines, choosing a seat next to her for the flight home. This would have been the common mistake made by people who assume, the more contact the better! But this story illustrates the definition of being appropriate in network building—**not putting the other person in an uncomfortable position by acting like the relationship is more substantial than it is in that moment in time.** And being appropriate, as I have noted, makes people feel comfortable with developing a closer relationship.

The story has a happy ending. I got to know the dean through further interactions, and eleven months later I taught my first class at the law school in "Arizona Legislative Process" as an adjunct professor. She invited me to speak on numerous panels in career programs at the law school. The dean even suggested I take a full-time job at the law school in the development office, which I appreciated but turned down because it did not dovetail with my career goals. During this time, we also became friendly and socialized together a bit before she moved on to a school in another state. And, while I learned an enormous amount from the experience of instructing a law school class for two years, I ultimately decided teaching was not for me and refocused my professional goals elsewhere.

This experience illustrates one of the greatest rewards of network building. In this situation, I began by wanting to meet the dean for a specific purpose. **I would not have had that opportunity were it not for the access to her that a member of my network facilitated.** It is humanly impossible to meet and show value to all the people in life whom you might ever wish to meet or seek help from, whether for a job, a scholarship, or a sale. The people in your network, though, are part of the interlinked webs of many other networks. Because you are a valuable member of *your* friends' networks, they will be willing to go the extra mile to introduce or recommend you to those other people. Why? Not because they like you, but because they are confident you will provide the same value to their contacts.

As you get to know their connections, you still must employ these relationship building skills and demonstrate value for two reasons. First, you want not only to achieve your goal (the promotion, the teaching position, etc.) but also to become a valued member of the new person's network. Second, you *must* reflect well on your own network member who facilitated the connection, in order to maintain your original relationship. Being appropriate is critical to both.

Note also in this story how many of my Tips came into play:

- First, I created value for everyone in this equation. Being good at my work allowed me to be a person who could be seriously considered for a law school teaching position. It was also the reason two lawyers in my network offered to introduce me to people who could help me explore teaching; both of them had seen the quality of my work when we practiced law together. By coming up with a program idea for the dean in her new role, I offered value to her in the form of an interesting idea and fresh perspective.

- Second, to initiate conversation with the dean, I figured out something we had in common to use as a starting point—our shared history at D.C. law schools.

- Third, my hobby of figure skating allowed me to have a fun and memorable conversation with the dean when I ran into her in the airport.

- Fourth, I followed up on my initial interaction with the dean with a handwritten note.

- Finally, I was appropriate in all interactions. I did not ask my network friends for help that would have made them uncomfortable; I asked them for information and they took the initiative to go that extra mile. I did not make the dean feel awkward by being intrusive or "sales-y" in any way.

Of course, the dean was not inspired to offer me the teaching gig solely because of my actions. As you would expect, she called around to members of the legal community who knew me. What clinched her decision was the endorsement by members of my network in that community who had seen me providing valuable, high quality work for years. Had those people not seen fit to enthusiastically recommend me, I would not have this story to tell. We can conclude once again: All roads lead back to Tip #1 – Be good at your job.

PUTTING IT INTO PRACTICE
TIP #9 – Be Appropriate in Your Follow-Up

Past: *As we discussed, it's often easier to see when someone is being inappropriate than it is when they are being appropriate. Think of a time when you saw someone request something professionally that seemed inappropriate. Maybe someone has requested something of you that made you uncomfortable because you barely knew them. Can you recall an occasion when you yourself did something inappropriate and regretted it later?*

Present: *Make sure the follow-up you do for this past week under Tip #8 is appropriate to the relationship you have with the person. If you just met them, a short email is perfect. If you enjoyed a great conversation with a colleague you are getting to know, or received help or support from someone, consider trying out the tactful coffee invitation.*

Future: *In Tip #8 you allocated a half hour at the end of each week for follow-up. Now, each week during this allocated time, make sure to consider the most appropriate way to do so. Think carefully about the way to make the best impression and not make the person you are following up with feel uncomfortable. What would you most appreciate if you were in their shoes?*

DO WHAT YOU CAN DO

TIP #10:

HELP THE PEOPLE IN YOUR NETWORK

As I hope I've driven home repeatedly throughout this book, the principle behind building a successful network is that you must show others why having you in *their* networks will add value for them. Although you are reading this book because you want to build a network of supportive friends and colleagues for your own benefit, you can do so only by being of value to others first. Once you have demonstrated your worth, however, you will strengthen your relationships if you continue to be a source of assistance.

Tip #10 is about consciously seeking opportunities to help members of your network. By now the members of your network have observed your value; that's why they already have added you to their own networks and why you have an ongoing relationship with them. Now, to maintain your network successfully, you must always be looking for a way to do something to help the people in your network—and then you must actually *do* it. This goes beyond the problem-solving you are doing for others at work by following Tip #1 and the value you are bringing to your organizations under Tip #3; think of it as "extra credit."

So how do you determine what it is you can do? First, ask yourself what it is about the other person that's interesting? What are their challenges, successes, problems and goals? People drop clues about these things into conversation all the time. Don't just listen for this information, process it. Do the same kind of analysis you do for Tip #1 when you are figuring out how to solve people's problems at work. Now, how can you step up and help your network members outside of your job?

You can be most successful at this if you literally change your way of listening. Try in every conversation to consciously identify something that would help the person you are talking to. I'm not suggesting that you always verbalize your conclusions during the conversation; I can safely say that no one wants constant unsolicited advice! But approach every conversation with the idea that you will try to identify—at least to yourself—one thing that you could do to help out the other person. Then, once you are alone, take a moment to reflect on and capture the opportunities that you spotted.

I am not recommending that you act on every observation. This newfound readiness to step forward will be applied only to people in your network and even then not all the time. Before you can take action, however, you have to see what help is needed, and listening with this approach is the way to do it. As a bonus, being a good listener is one more quality that will endear you to members of your network.

I once met a nice woman in a sailing class who told me this story. She and her two siblings decided to quit their jobs and start a family business manufacturing furniture. The business was quickly successful, and a year after opening they needed to move to a new, larger location. The three decided to close shop for a few days and undertake the chore themselves.

A few days beforehand, one of their suppliers called, wanting to schedule a delivery during that time. The trio told him they would be closed in order to relocate, and asked him to delay delivery for a week. **On the Saturday morning of the move, this supplier surprised them by showing up at their warehouse with his truck.** He volunteered to help and spent the entire day sweating alongside the siblings as they transferred to the new location.

This man is one of my relationship-building idols. Instead of listening from only his perspective ("Darn, they're closed, I'll have to change my schedule to make the delivery next week, how inconvenient for me."), he listened from theirs. He then made considerable personal sacrifice— manual labor *and* a whole day away from his other work—to support them. Do you think this woman and her siblings *ever* bought materials from any other supplier again? I doubt it.

I am lucky that listening this way came naturally to me early on. I have honed this skill even further over the years by actively working on it and doing the exercise that I mentioned above. The idea for help that you come up with does not have to be elaborate, complex, or even difficult. You do not have to go for the big, dramatic gesture. If the person is suffering renal failure, donating a kidney is not your only option. Information and referrals are always appreciated whether they are used or not.

Recently I had breakfast with a bank executive from out of state who is in my network. I had gotten to know him through serving with him on the board of directors of a business group. He had just bought a vacation home in my city and was here to visit his new place. I asked him to breakfast because I wanted to pick his brain about potential client opportunities for me in his industry, possibly even within his own bank.

During breakfast he mentioned that he was looking for a handyman to maintain his vacation home in his absence and asked me if I knew anyone. I said regretfully that I did not. But, I heard his problem and decided to help. I offered to call friends who I knew lived in the area of his new home and ask them if they knew a handyman. After breakfast I spent some time on the phone, and by the next day had found him someone who came highly recommended.

By the way, even though I found him a handyman, my bank executive friend did not offer any suggestions regarding contracts for me in his industry—and that's okay. Relationship building is not transactional. Not everyone will be able to or even want to help you every time. You will have missed the point of this Tip if you go into each interaction looking for ways to help someone in exchange for them doing something for you.

I was on the receiving end of help from my network during the Coronavirus pandemic. I had called a network friend to ask how she and her family were doing during the shutdown. As we talked, we laughed ruefully about the dearth of certain items in grocery stores. I mentioned that I had an upcoming plane trip and had been unsuccessfully on the hunt for disinfecting wipes—a scarce and coveted item at the time—to take along.

The next day my friend called to tell me she had seen wipes while shopping and, remembering our conversation, had bought some for me as a gift for my trip. You can see that my friend was following the precept of really listening as we talked, hearing what I needed, and taking action to solve my problem. I am so grateful to be in her network!

When to act

Tip #10 is not about doing things for others constantly and indiscriminately. Once you have begun to identify the assistance that others need, how do you choose when to step forward and help?

I mentioned in the previous chapter that people will put themselves on the line only for others who they think are worth it. This is why you want to add value, or "worth," to the lives of those in your network. It is human nature for the members of your network to subconsciously evaluate how "worth it" it will be for them to help you. They will act consistently with that evaluation. The greater the cost or effort involved, the more "worth it" it must be to your network members to act. This, by the way, is why asking for information is always an appropriate way to seek assistance, since it usually requires little effort on the part of the ask-ee to accommodate the request.

Helping someone get a job or obtain a new client, on the other hand, requires more investment of time and resources and may place the helper's own reputation at stake. To receive this kind of assistance from those in your network you must be valuable enough to them to be worth it —the basis for this entire book. **This same principle applies in reverse when you follow Tip #10 and offer help to others.**

As you demonstrate value to more and more people, your network of relationships will grow. Your new friends, however, may not offer the same level of value in return—and that's okay. Keep in mind that when you meet someone you do not know whether they will have significance in your life. Also recall that you are not focusing only on building relationships with "important" people (Tip #6). But, when it comes to following the advice of this chapter and helping those in your network, you must be sure that the level of assistance you offer is "worth it" to you.

Most people can instinctively decide how much of their time and energy to make available to someone else. When it comes to potential impact on your reputation, however, thoughtfully consider how best to proceed. By now, if you are following the Tips in this book, your network friends will trust your recommendations and advice. Because *you* are valuable to them, they will assume that you will connect them only with others who also are valuable. They will believe you if you tell them that Julie is the best candidate for the open position in their department, or that Joe will give them the best customer service if his company is hired to provide all the steel beams for their construction projects. If Julie and Joe do not perform as advertised, however, *you* are the one whose value and credibility will be in doubt.

So what do you do when Julie, a fellow board member from your professional marketers society, asks you about the opening at your company in the marketing department? Although she's a fun and friendly person, Julie has not been a terrific board member. You have observed that she doesn't show up to half the meetings and is rarely prepared when she does. As much as you like her, you cannot be sure that Julie would be a great employee if she came to work with you. If you recommend Julie to the head of the department and she interviews poorly, or worse, is hired and is mediocre, your co-workers will conclude that you have poor judgment and your company may suffer. What to do?

If Julie simply requests information about the position, your problem is solved. You can cheerfully provide her with the job description and information about how to apply and keep it at that. If she asks you to recommend her, however, what then? This is where you must determine how "worth it" it is to you to place your own reputation on the line to help Julie. Maybe she is the person who nominated you for the marketing society board in the first place. Maybe you barely know her. Maybe in addition to being a fellow board member she is also your sister-in-law. Maybe she once pulled you from a burning car crash. My point here is that when your actions will affect others' perception of *your* value, you should consider all factors before deciding how "worth it" it is, or how far you are willing to go, to help someone. The final decision is up to you.

If you choose to recommend Julie, do *not* overstate her abilities. Be straightforward about the reasons you are recommending her. Tell your company that she is a fun and friendly person who has helped you at the marketing society. If Julie once saved your life, ask the HR department for the personal favor to you of granting her an interview since she is the reason you're still on this earth. Do not ascribe outstanding professional qualities to her. If you do and she is hired and performs poorly, you will be known by all as a person with poor judgment.

On the other hand, if you don't want to endorse Julie, there is nothing wrong with telling her you will see what you can find out. Then, track down some information for her about the job and the company. Maybe offer her the bio of the person who will be conducting interviews, if that's not confidential information. You are responding to her request for assistance, it's just with assistance of a different kind. If Julie later asks you outright if you put in a good word for her, you can tell her that the opportunity did not arise. You have been helpful and kind to a member of your network without causing harm to your own relationships. And remember: If Julie had put in the effort to show value at the marketing society, this entire discussion would be unnecessary.

When the relationships involved are based on value, a situation like the one above plays out very differently. Last year a member of my network asked me if I knew of a job for her daughter's friend Kaitlyn who had recently graduated from college. My network friend assured me that although Kaitlyn was young and inexperienced, she was a rising star and would be an asset anywhere she worked. Because my friend has outstanding judgment and is a superstar in her own right, I was immediately comfortable calling a client of mine to recommend Kaitlyn for an entry-level opening in their communications department. I told my client that even though I did not know Kaitlyn personally, I had so much confidence in my network friend that I was willing to make the call. Kaitlyn was quickly hired from a pool of more than forty applicants. Last I heard she was excelling in her new role.

How to help

If a specific activity does not suggest itself, providing information is generally a good option to help members of your network. Offering information that may beneficially connect two people who already are acquainted or work in the same place is often welcome. Frequently people are not aware that someone they already know could be a valuable resource to them.

It also can be rewarding to offer information to new acquaintances who may be potential future network members. Earlier this year I had an appointment with a senator at our state capitol. His assistant Karla was new, and as I waited in the antechamber for my meeting, I asked her where she had worked before coming to the capitol. (Sound familiar as a conversational gambit? See Tip #4 – Get to know people at your new group.) She replied that she was in school getting her Master's degree in Social Work. Her capitol work was temporary; she hoped to get a job in her own field upon graduation. I immediately responded by informing her that another senator at the capitol actually was a social worker in his "day job." Perhaps she could learn useful career information by talking with him.

Later that day I made it a point to seek out the social worker senator. I told him about Karla and suggested he have a conversation with her to offer her career guidance. He gladly agreed, saying he would enjoy the chance to talk about his field. I circled back to Karla and told her to call him. Hopefully they talked and she got some useful ideas or connections to help her in her job search. Even if she didn't, she no doubt appreciated my effort to help her out.

Sometimes your network friends will ask you if you can introduce them to someone you know whom they want to meet. If they have read this book, they will know to ask you for information about that person rather than directly for an introduction itself ("I understand you're friends with Jim, the head of global sales at Acme Consulting; what would be a good way for me to meet him to talk about breaking into European markets?"). This allows you to respond by providing the level of help that you feel comfortable with: Answering with the information requested, or, if you are enthusiastic about your network friend's value, a call to Jim to suggest the connection.

Network friends who have yet to read this book, however, may ask you directly for an introduction to Jim. Just as in the example about Julie the marketing professional, you must evaluate how making this introduction will reflect on you. Will Jim enjoy or find value in meeting your network friend? Or, realistically, will it be something Jim does only as a favor for you, with no benefit to him? (Think back to the lunch I agreed to have with the husband of the chamber of commerce media director only because I valued *her* as a member of my network.) Is Jim a Big Deal who is besieged daily by requests for introductions? Also, how important to you is your network friend and how far are you willing to go for him? Thoughtfully assessing these questions will help you decide if it is "worth it" to you to connect these two people.

You do not have to do big things to make a big difference for someone in your network. When I ran a trade association, I used to host an annual "Day at the Legislature" for my members. One year I arrived early and stationed myself on the sidewalk in front of the capitol, so that I could greet my members as they arrived from the parking lot and direct them to our meeting room. As I stood there, I realized that my breath was, shall we say, less than fresh. Since it was about 8:30 in the morning, many lobbyists and staff were arriving at the legislature as well, and I began to ask the ones I knew if they had a piece of gum or a breath mint. I got lots of regretful shakes of the head, and a couple of "That's rough!" comments, especially once I explained that I couldn't leave my post to go find mints because I was awaiting my visitors.

I had just decided that I would simply have to keep my mouth shut until I could take a break later when I felt a tap on my shoulder. One of the lobbyists whom I had asked, although empty-handed on his way in, had heard my plea. He had gone into the capitol to the basement vending machines, purchased a roll of mint Lifesavers, and come back outside to deliver them to me. His outlay: fifty cents and five minutes. My gratitude: eternal. I'm still telling this story twenty years later.

You will not always be in a position to save the day for your network contacts. But, you can see how powerful moments like these can be. Think about what you can do for your network contacts; it can be an opportunity to build lifelong devotion.

A final thought on helping your network members. (You knew this was coming, right?) **There is no more important value than Tip #1, being good at your job.** A recent trend among "networking" gurus is to offer a version of Tip #10 as the single modern-day means by which to build relationships. This advice is cloaked in the virtue of generosity: Figure out what others want and give it to them! Listen sympathetically, connect them to important people, give them gifts, and you will add them to your network. Easy, right? Wrong.

Tip #10 is last in this book for a reason. Only with the foundation laid by following Tip #1 and the other previous Tips will your value to others be intrinsic, that is, a part of who you are. Attempting to lure others into your network by giving them things—sporting event tickets, fancy dinners, monogrammed portfolio covers—may seem to work at first, but once you stop the flow of benefits, you have nothing to hold them there. Oh, some of those people may feel obliged to reciprocate, but you will not create meaningful, authentic relationships. Your newfound friends will be there for the goodies, not for you.

The same is true of offering the benefit of introductions to important people you may know. Your important-people friends may not welcome your relationship with them being used in barter to entice new people to add you to their networks. Even if the introduction is worthwhile, if you are not of value yourself, once your two friends connect you may find yourself slowly fading from the picture.

If the value you offer to others is your own bedrock professionalism as a reliable job performer and outstanding problem solver, people will want you in their networks even if you never give them so much as a paper clip. Tip #10, helping the members of your network, is about enhancing the value you provide, not creating it. **It helps characterize your relationships as the kind in which you come to each other's aid.** If you have followed Tip #1 and have intrinsic value, you are someone with whom others want to have that kind of relationship.

PUTTING IT INTO PRACTICE
TIP #10 – Help the People in Your Network

Past: *Remember a time somebody did something unexpected to support you and it made a big difference in your day, or week, or life. Have you ever stepped up and helped a friend or colleague without them having to ask?*

Present: *This week as you talk to people you consider to be in your network, listen to see if you can find just one thing to do for one of them that would help them out or ease their stress—then do it.*

Future: *If you created a checklist under Tip #1, add to it, or create one now. Add the action item of listening carefully when you talk to members of your network for ways you could help them—and check it off daily if you listened that way in even just one conversation. Once you begin to regularly come up with ideas to help, choose one or two and do them. Never forget, when an action may reflect on **you**, consider that impact before you proceed.*

TO THINE OWN SELF BE TRUE

BONUS TIP:
BE SINCERE

There may be readers who, at some point along the way, start to wonder if following these Tactical Tips means they are being "fake." As someone who has made a living for the past thirty years from my relationship-building skills, I can emphatically say that this is being fake only if *you* are fake. For you to succeed at making meaningful connections—or any other life goal, in my opinion—you must be sincere. You must solve other people's problems because you genuinely want to help them. You must be nice to people because you want to be, and do things for them from a place in your heart of generosity. You must ask them questions about their backgrounds and interests because you truly want to know the answers, not because a book told you to do so.

The following guideline will help you stay sincere: Don't try to build a relationship with anyone you don't like. I don't mean you shouldn't be courteous and respectful of others. I also don't mean that you should avoid interacting with anyone that you don't agree with. We all have had the experience in our lives of working with people we don't care for, or people who we think are jerks. Often, spending time with them is not optional. For some unfortunate people, those are their bosses. There are plenty of books about dealing with bad bosses or getting along with toxic people. This is not one of them.

My point is, if you meet someone and don't like them, then don't make an effort to build a relationship with them (beyond following Tip #1, of course—always be good at your job!). First impressions can change, but I am talking about those (hopefully few) people out there who grate on you, who you don't click with, or who you don't respect.

Once in my early days as a lobbyist, there was a public official whom I disliked for a number of reasons. The problem was that this official, a single woman like me, was new to my state and was in search of friends. She perceived us as having a lot in common and tried to befriend me, inviting me to lunch and suggesting weekend activities. It would have been very beneficial to my work to have this woman think of me as a friend. But I felt guilty and uncomfortable at the idea of pretending to be her pal for the purpose of professional gain while secretly disliking her. Therefore I made excuses to turn down the lunch invitations and the weekend jaunts, while remaining courteous and outwardly friendly in the workplace. Eventually she stopped asking and my integrity remained intact.

Many of the Tips in this book would be equally helpful if your only goal was making new friends for social purposes, like my retired colleague in Tip #5 who knew no one in her new city. I once came across a thoughtful little pamphlet for pre-teens with ideas about how to make friends. It suggested sharing, being a good listener, doing what the other person wants to do some of the time, and being willing to give less popular kids a second look as potential friends. Would you dismiss a child's friendship as somehow not genuine because it was gained by intentionally following these precepts?

You might notice that throughout this book I refer to those in my network as "friends." That's because of a simple fact: I consider each person in my network to be a friend. This doesn't mean everyone in my network is my BFF or that I spend time with all of them away from work. It does mean that I sincerely care about them and appreciate the value they bring to my life, whether our paths cross weekly or once a decade. It also means that I treat them like friends and hope they feel the same way about me.

There is a critical distinction, however, between making friends and building relationships for professional success. It is often said that people do business with people they like. I agree that being liked is important, and it is one of the reasons I exhort you in Tip #3 to be easy to get along with when you join organizations. (It probably wouldn't hurt to be that way all the time.) But, as we discussed in Tip #4, the best network is made up of more than just people who feel warmly toward you. The most rewarding and fulfilling relationships are with people who will assist you in time of need and who will give of themselves and their resources to help you, **because you are valuable to them**.

Let's face it, we all have friends who, to put it kindly, have failed to reach their full potential. These folks may even be our dearest friends. But think back to the dilemma in Tip #10 of helping Julie, the marketing society colleague. Be honest: Would you try to help your dear friend get a great job or a great promotion if their subsequent poor performance could possibly hurt your chances for professional success? Even if admirable loyalty to your old high school pal Jack causes you to waver in your answer, the reality is that people most want to help others who are professionally capable. In order to be part of someone's meaningful network, you must offer a value proposition beyond just being liked.

Another way to stay sincere is to not force yourself to engage in activities you dislike because you are committed to meeting people. For example, I developed a great group of network friends over the years serving on the board of directors for a trade association. The group was based in another state, and I enjoyed traveling to see my colleagues on a regular basis at the bimonthly meetings. But each evening after the official group dinner, when everyone headed to the bar for late night boisterous fun, I would excuse myself and go to my hotel room. I loved the people, but as an introvert my tolerance for group gatherings is limited, and I'm an early bird who doesn't like staying up late. Did this affect the quality of my relationships with these individuals? Not at all.

Some of you introverts are thinking, I dislike all of the activities you recommend! You have probably made it to the end of this book, however, because you realize that you need to take some deliberate action to develop a network. You want to build these satisfying and rewarding relationships in your professional life. The principles I have laid out here illustrate that you can build a network without engaging in the dreaded activity of approaching total strangers you may never see again and trying to make conversation. Maybe my proffered change in approach is an opportunity for you to enjoy meeting people after all. Why not do yourself a favor and be open to it?

Sometimes after I speak to a group on the subject of building a network, people will come up to me afterward and say that everything I told them to do is already obvious. (Fortunately for my ego this is usually part of commentary about how much they enjoyed my remarks.) But if it is so obvious, why is it such a rarity to find people who do these things? The truth is that we are all caught up in ourselves and our goals, both for getting through life and for getting through the day. We want to be more successful at our work, with our families, in our lives in general, and we hunger for information about how to make that happen for ourselves. We are not used to considering our own interaction with the world from someone else's perspective.

My disdain for traditional "networking" is this: In practice I find it describes a selfish, self-centered focus on meeting other people in order to obtain one's own goals as quickly as possible while completely ignoring the fact that the other person has goals too. I said at the beginning of this book that I believe the world would be a better place if everyone took my approach to building relationships, instead of embracing the traditional methods of "networking." After all, when you are truly following the Core Principle of being the kind of person others want to have in their networks, you are living the Golden Rule. Be the person you wish others would be.

A FINAL CHALLENGE: HAVE FUN!

I will close with a final piece of advice: enjoy yourself! Yes, have fun as you pursue the creation of a network of friends and colleagues who will support you all of your days. Take pleasure in excelling, exceeding expectations, getting to know new people, trying new activities, indulging in your hobbies, and learning about new organizations. Now that you are not frantically "selling" yourself during "networking" activities, you can slow down, take a deep breath, and just enjoy other people. The old adage is true: Life is a journey, and it is made richer by what happens along the way.

By following the Tactical Tips I have given you here, you will build lifelong relationships. The people you meet will enrich your life, and you will enrich theirs. Cheerleaders will encourage and support you along the road to professional success, and you will make a difference in the lives of many others. What are you waiting for?

ABOUT THE AUTHOR

Ellen Poole teaches people at all levels of their careers effective strategies to build networks and nurture relationships for professional success. Her audiences have included nationwide corporate teams, law students, and state, local and international professional and trade associations.

After graduating from the George Washington University Law School, Poole moved cross country to practice law in Arizona. Despite knowing almost no one when she arrived in her new, adopted state, within six years she had become the fourth woman in U.S. history to be chosen as CEO of a state bankers association and was named by the *Phoenix Business Journal* as one of its ten most influential people under 40. More recently, Poole spent almost 15 years as a multi-state government relations executive for Fortune 100 company USAA, where she built a professional network spanning the country. She also has worked for the Arizona state legislature and is a graduate of Virginia Tech.

Poole's success with a unique approach to building relationships puts a new spin on the meaning of "network"—and how to build and sustain strong and meaningful relationships in business and in life.

ACKNOWLEDGMENTS

I want to start by thanking Karen Hale, who was the first person to suggest that I speak on the subject of "networking" when she invited me to talk to her corporate team, and Brett Dawson, who, after voluntarily subjecting himself several times to my presentations, said to me one day, "You should write a book." Their encouragement started me on this journey.

I must give a special note of gratitude to my friend Wayne Peacock. For years he has inspired me to meet high standards; even after we no longer worked together I would often ask myself what Wayne would expect whenever I engaged in any professional pursuit. His glowing Foreword for this book is an incredible validation of my work and my ideas about professional relationship building. Thank you for your confidence in me, Wayne.

This book wouldn't be a reality without the help of Mona Gambetta of Brisance Book Group and Isha Cogborn of Epiphany Institute. Appreciation also goes to Marty Latz of the Latz Negotiation Institute for putting me on the right path and his patience in answering my many questions.

Last, I must mention my parents. My mom Karin Poole is a dynamo at age 83 and inspires me to daily optimism about what lies ahead in life. My father Arthur S. Poole Jr. is no longer with us, but ever since I was a little girl he thought I could do anything. I know he would be very proud of this book.

END NOTES | BACK COVER OF DUST JACKET

LinkedIn Global Survey Results, *Eighty-percent of professionals consider networking important to career success* (Jun 22, 2017) https://news.linkedin.com/2017/6/eighty-percent-of-professionals-consider-networking-important-to-career-success

Casciaro, Gino & Kouchaki, *The Contaminating Effects of Building Instrumental Ties: How Networking Can Make Us Feel Dirty* (Oct 6, 2014) https://doi.org/10.1177/0001839214554990